TIM CROC

Developing Yourself as a Leader

Becoming a Leader: Everything they forgot to tell you in school and how you can learn it!

Tim Crocker

Dedication

This book is dedicated to all of the young men and women now entering the work force, starting their professions, and growing their careers. I hope for them the same mentorships and opportunities that I have had the benefit of over the years. To all of them I say never forget to give something back to another when you have the chance.

In addition, I dedicate this book to my daughter Yuri who never ceases to both amaze and fascinate me with her optimistic view of the world, resilient personality, and emotional intelligence.

Tim

Table of Contents

1. FORWARD 3
2. INTRODUCTION 4
3. GOLDEN RULES 6
4. ADVICE TO THE NEW MANAGER 8
5. LEADERSHIP FUNDAMENTALS 21
6. GOALS AND MOTIVATION 27
7. INTRODUCTION TO CONTINUOUS IMPROVEMENT 38
8. PROBLEM-SOLVING BASICS 55
9. LEARNING THE ART OF DELEGATION 64
10. SERVANT LEADERSHIP 75
11. COMMUNICATION: HABITS, BEHAVIORS, AND EXPECTATIONS 87
12. WHY YOU MUST POINT OUT WHAT "GOOD" LOOKS LIKE 92
13. INTRODUCTION TO THE CHANGE CURVE 95
14. BUILDING A CULTURE OF TEAM ACCOUNTABILITY 101
15. TIPS FOR MORE PRODUCTIVE COACHING 105
16. BUILDING TEAM TRUST AND THE SAFE SPACE ...112
17. INTRODUCTION TO PROJECT BASICS AND AVOIDING FAILURE...118

18	THE VALUE OF BOARD SERVICE	134
19	BREAKING YOUR BAD HABITS BEFORE THEY BUST YOUR CAREER	142
20	AVOIDING JOB BURN OUT	149
21	DO I WANT A JOB OR A CAREER	157
22	CONCLUSION	167

1 FORWARD

It's not often in life one gets asked to write a Forward for a book. I consider it both an honor and an opportunity to reinforce the message you are about to experience. Tim Crocker's quest to put to paper his practical advice and "to the point" guidance on managing and organization provides an incredible road map for new and experienced managers. As I was reading it and thinking it through, it hit me that if I were to be truthfully honest with myself, I could use it in a "check list" approach, first as a self-assessment, then as a roadmap to chart my own pathway to improvement. It is just that practical and useful and, knowing Tim, that's just the type of leader he is. Get to the facts, get to the point and execute,…. but in a way that brings people along with his journey. Build a team that succeeds and believes in themselves. That, my friend, is the hallmark of great leadership, bringing the organization along the journey. What else are you waiting for?

Carey A. Buckles

36 years in Chemical Manufacturing Operations, Technology Development, Engineering Dow, NatureWorks, BP, StoraEnso, WR Grace

2 INTRODUCTION

If you are reading this, I must first say thank you. I appreciate your interest in taking this opportunity to listen to the ideas that I have gathered in this body of work. I have grown and have benefitted considerably, from not only my own years in the workplace but also, from a greater degree, the wise council and advice of those more experienced than myself. This book is an attempt at transferring some of that knowledge to you, along with making you aware of a few key books you might use on your own to deepen your skills and abilities in a particular area.

The intent of this book is for you to read at you own pace front to back. Each chapter is self-contained, enabling you to bounce between certain topics at your leisure, depending upon your particular area of interest. Every chapter has some suggested reading that I consider a minimum to learn the basic principles of each subject area.

The intent of each chapter is simply to function as a brief introduction to each topic. Only the "30,000 foot" view of the area is presented. Every chapter references a few books that teach the fundamentals of the topic in detail. My goal is not to cover any topic comprehensively, but rather to give you the briefest introduction, provide a few study assignments and exercises, and provide you with the logical in-depth references if you are interested in exploring that subject area exhaustively.

Each chapter has clear learning objectives. Most chapters have some detailed exercises that are intended to be thought provoking and enable the reader to both understand the material and apply the principles into their daily lives. Beyond this there are provided in every chapter suggested reading that can be used to study more deeply into specific areas.

Embrace change. Become a lifelong learner.

Read.

Enjoy.

Tim

3 GOLDEN RULES

Learning Objective

1. Become familiar with some basic rules that will drive your success

These basic rules of thumb are important enough they need to have their own chapter.

1. Communicate face to face – never write an email to someone who is within walking distance.
2. Never be late to a meeting. If you are presenting be early and have all your equipment working.
3. Never complain about leadership – it always gets back to them.
4. Be fully professional in all correspondence and never reply to all.
5. Always respect chain of command.
6. Dress and speak every day as if you were interviewing for you job.
7. Do not hold a grudge – start every day new. Be the person who overlooks snubs from others.
8. Admit you mistakes.
9. Be honest.
10. Be careful with posting on social media.
11. Identify and concentrate on the critical few decisions.
12. A call is better than no call.
13. Give your decisions a short leash. Quickly pull back in case of mistake.

14. Trust your intuition.
15. Get feedback early and often and act on this feedback.
16. Earn the trust and confidence of others.
17. Demonstrate vulnerability to gain credibility.
18. Play to your strengths.

Exercises

1. Not to revel in the missteps of others – but make note this week when you see a coworker take an action that could have been done more effectively. Does it correspond to one of the rules?
2. Think of a time when you had a situation go badly and how could you have handled it differently?
3. Based on your experiences what "rules" would you propose? Write down and develop your own list. These can become your personal "brand".

Suggested Reading

The Rules of Work: A definitive code for personal success, by Richard Templar

4 ADVICE TO THE NEW MANAGER

Learning Objectives

1. The rule of 4.
2. How to meet a new team.
3. How to start new relationships with an entire team.

If you are a newly promoted manager, you will go through a phase of uncertainty as you build your new team. This is true for even the most experienced leader. Every new unit or department will bring unique challenges.

Your first day on the job will significantly influence your success as a manager. In some cases, day one may determine whether you are successful or not in your new position. Remember that what has worked with one group of employees in another department, unit, or industry is not necessarily a predictor of success in a new environment.

Without exception, the successful manager is one who fosters an environment conducive to productivity and creativity. Conversely, the less-than-successful manager wields an authoritative manner, which often creates a sense of general unease. A climate of unease, distrust, or fear is likely to be neither productive nor creative.

Creating this work environment is possible for every manager. It requires that you embrace two important principles:

1. Lead from the heart. Show an interest in employee well-being; keep your commitments; value their time like your own; empower every individual. Listen to opinions of your team; respect what they have to say; put their career development and opportunities ahead of your own.

2. Practice the Rule of 4. A new team or a new team member typically requires about four times longer to become engaged and to produce the same results than a veteran employee does. Expect a slower pace and anticipate the need to, at least initially, communicate basic principles often.

There is a fine line between setting clear expectations and micro-managing. Your success as a manager depends on finding a balance during the first few weeks on the job. Get to know your team and identify their strengths and weaknesses. Set your own goals and empower every member of your team to set both short and long-term goals.

"You will never get a second chance to make a first impression". --Will Rogers

Meet and Greet

The structure of your organization may dictate the circumstances of your first contact with your new employees. Some organizations may prefer to have someone higher in management introduce new managers to their work teams. Other organizations may prefer to have the new manager work out the details of meeting the new team.

If you are meeting your work team on your own, it is essential to have an introduction plan.

1. Schedule an introduction meeting. Ensure that everyone attending knows the time and place at least a week in advance. Establish an agenda and state the purpose of the meeting.
2. When possible, have a recognizable company leader introduce you. If not, introduce yourself.
3. Highlight only the relevant job experience you have had. Avoid talking about your accomplishments. Leaders who talk only about their successes may be perceived as boastful and egotistical.
4. Instead of dwelling on what you have already accomplished, focus, instead, on your plans for your shared success.
5. Stress the concept of shared success.
6. Take some time to show your human side. Share personal or family interests. Let your team know that you personally balance work and home life. Be mindful that there is a limit to personal sharing. Use common sense in what kind and how much detail you share.
7. Listen to your team. Take notes whenever any individual speaks. Give everyone an opportunity to voice an opinion.

Set Goals

In the One-Minute Manager, Ken Blanchard identifies the first "minute task:" one-minute goal setting. Before setting large or multiple goals, however, start with an overview and break goals into stages and "complete-able" actions.

In order to set goals collaboratively with your team, you must practice active listening. The best way to listen actively is to keep the multi-tasking to a bare minimum when interacting with team members. An active listener retains approximately 60% of pertinent information. Multi-taskers retain approximately 30%.

Your purpose is to get to know your team, to build a culture of inclusiveness, and to establish team and project expectations. You want to hear as much as possible. Show your team the importance of paying attention by paying attention to them.

Building a climate of trust requires that everyone listen and attend to others' contributions. When responding to an employee's idea or suggestion, if you're tempted to say "no," replace with "yes, and?" Avoid judging an idea on impulse. If there is possibility the idea has merit, you don't want to have missed the opportunity. You never know where a conversation may lead, and the words no and but are likely to immediately end any further conversation on the topic. Being consistently negative will ensure that your employees avoid taking risks by sharing their ideas.

"To lead people, walk behind them." ---Lao Tsu

Know Your People

As a manager, you want to know your people well. It may seem more efficient to simply place people you have worked with into the key roles on your team; by doing this, however, you risk overlooking outstanding talent.

Get to know your people. Review their files and know something about their histories. Be observant. Identify key influencers on the team; they can assist others with buy-in. If you are taking over an already-formed team, key influencers are essential to managing the group effectively.

Set aside time to chat -- and to listen. Discover what key influencers think. Learn what drives them.

Just as identifying key influencers is important, so, too, is determining who the natural leader of the group is. By practicing active listening and observing team interaction, you can learn whom the group avoids, who swings the group opinion, who mentors the group when a problem arises, and who the natural leader of the group is.

Create your Change Coalition

Change is inevitable when a new manager picks up the reins. And change is often a real challenge to existing teams. Research suggests that in any given established group, about 10% of the individuals affected enthusiastically embrace the change. About 10% of any given group strongly resists change. The 80% in the middle require reasons to change – and the reasons are not necessarily always logical reasons. They are comfortable with the status quo and see no need to change. Key influencers in this group do not necessarily fall into the enthusiastic 10% or the resistant 10%. As a part of the 80% in the middle, they may have the potential to influence the team, but they may not be the people you want as a part of your change coalition.

Begin by identifying early on reliable and consistent people whom you want to make up your change coalition. In order to ensure buy-in from your entire team, make sure everyone understands expectations prior to rolling out any changes in the way the team is managed. Clearly identify objectives when announcing changes, and reiterate the objectives at the end of the rollouts to make sure everyone is on the same page and has a clear understanding of the changes.

Once any changes or plans have been announced, follow up with an email to ensure that the entire team knows you are available to discuss the changes. Make sure that any team member was not present when the rollout was announced is informed of all proposed changes. Invite them to discuss their opinions with you. Address any issues the nay-sayers may have with the proposed change or the team goals. Ignoring problems will only exacerbate them.

Effective managers lead by example; they are undaunted in the face of anxiety and uncertainty; they show positive results from embracing change. Managers who do this well create trust within their teams. Without trust, fostering change will be a real struggle.

Efficient managers are transparent. They talk openly of change. They celebrate their team's successes in embracing change and resolving problems. During significant times of change, anxiety is easily created by a lack of information. Closing the information gap prevents people from creating their own versions of reality, which are, oftentimes, much more negative than actual reality.

"A leader is one who knows the way, goes the way, and shows the way". ---John Maxwell

Follow Through

Leaders are responsible for making things happen. They deliver what they commit to within budget and on time.

In order to build and maintain your team's trust, you must commit to an effective follow through. This establishes credibility and engenders trust. New managers often forget this key element and fail to make a positive impact because of it.

When things don't happen as promised, employees lose faith and become discouraged. If they cannot see tangible results, then their motivation to work is diminished. Effective managers follow through on commitments and ensure that goals are met and tasks are completed.

Nurture Relationships

One reason companies lose employees is placing profit ahead of team or employee relationships as their number one priority. Good working relationships must be a priority. A new manager should focus on building and maintaining employee relationships, not generating income. Income and profits result from good relationships. Developing courteous, professional working relationships pays off for everyone. The ability to develop strong relationships with peers and team members is an invaluable skill.

Communication and transparency are essential to strong team building. The effective manager will discuss issues and resolve difficulties as soon as they become apparent. Issues that arise should be dealt with constructively to avoid disruptions. Addressing issues as they arise will provide opportunities to make principle-based decisions and demonstrate your commitments and priorities to your team. Postponing an opportunity to address and resolve issues can often create bigger problems and undermine camaraderie.

Most problems can be resolved through open, honest communication. Regardless of their job title, all employees deserve respect and recognition for the work they do. Ensuring that all employees are heard will enable you to establish good relationships, build strong alliances, and foster a basic culture of trust and respect.

"Leaders don't create followers. They create more leaders."
---Tom Peters

Create Succession Planning from the Start

Successful companies know the value of having a back-up plan. To ensure that processes and production can continue seamlessly should a key employee suddenly become ill effective managers develop employees to fill key roles well in advance.

Successful planning becomes part of everyone's daily work. It drives work assignments and sets personal performance goals. It is, however, possible that companies or divisions undergoing significant change may let development of employees fall to the wayside. For example, transitioning into a new type of business may engender anxiety if employees are not trained with the proper skill set or if the type of work they are expected to perform is unfamiliar.

The successful manager will put processes in place to prepare people for organizational change. Managers can ensure uninterrupted production by delegating assignments, bubbling employees, and on-the-job shadowing. Everyone should stretch a little in these goals so that they are aiming for the expectations of the level above them.

Employees are "bubbled" when they are sent to another job or location where they work with peers to learn the job well enough to perform it on their own.

Some examples of this are preparation coverage during vacations, delegation assignments (bubble assignments), and shadowing, which enable the employee not only to understand the individual jobs within the unit, but also to gain insight into the operation as a whole.

Strong succession planning requires that employees are constantly developed so that key positions can be covered if the occasion arises. Succession planning also fosters upward mobility and opportunities within the team. As positions higher in the organization chart become available, employees who have been prepared can step easily into these positions.

As a successful manager, you will benefit from having an employee who can step into your role in your absence. Having a suitable replacement in mind also frees you up to consider moving up in the company should an opportunity arise. Often a good manager is passed over for promotions solely because they have no clear successor on the team.

Cross-training enables employees to expand their skills and provides an opportunity for them to explore other job possibilities. This can aid them in refining their personal and professional goals and keeps them realistic. Effective managers know their employees' professional goals. Knowing their career goals helps you to understand what drives them. Good managers sincerely want what is best for their employees.

The benefits of cross-training and succession planning are invaluable. The unit benefits by having seamless operations; the manager benefits by knowing that employees can migrate among positions when needed; and employees benefit by the exponential increase of skills and knowledge. Employees benefit from knowing the manager has confidence in their ability to keep production on schedule. Employees who believe their managers care about their well-being are likely to reciprocate that with loyalty and excellent work.

The best leader is the one who has sense enough to pick good men to do what he wants done and the self-restraint to keep from meddling with them while they do it. --Theodore Roosevelt

Recap

1. Start on the right foot. People form opinions rapidly and tend to stick with their initial thoughts. Take the time upfront to figure out how to get the team working well.
2. Get to know your team members and build camaraderie
3. Gain an early win that is a "team win."
4. Keep an open door.
5. Put your team first, yourself last.

6. Showcase your values. Make principle-based decisions. Explain the values and how you apply them.
7. Share your decision-making methodology.
8. Build teamwork. Explain what teamwork means.
9. Do not assume anything is understood.
10. Meet with your reports about four times more often than you might think is needed. Make the time to meet with them about twice as long as you think it should be. If your initial thought is "I will talk with each team member once a month for 30 minutes," start out with one hour a week, every week, with each team member. After you break through into real communication you can adjust. Over time you will learn to realize when you reach this point.

Take Aways

- ✓ Take the time to start out right.
- ✓ Over-communicate.
- ✓ Explain your values and principles.
- ✓ Aim for an early team win.
- ✓ Nurture relationships.
- ✓ Create succession planning right from the start.

Exercises

Take some time to reflect on your past and present work experiences to examine what best practices are already parts of your skill set.

1. Write 1,000 words about your favorite boss from the past. Why did you like him/her? What did he/she do in order to bolster your relationship? What can you incorporate into your style?
2. Make a list of how you would like to introduce yourself to your new team.
3. Make a list on your first day of your key-influencers. This can and will change over time.
4. Make a list of your change coalition.
5. Rate your relationships with your team members after your first week.

   1) I don't know and haven't talked to them at all.
   2) I know a bit about them.
   3) I have talked a lot with this person.
   4) This person has my trust.

When you are done rating your relationships with your team members, develop a plan to move people from 1-4.

Further Reading

One-Minute Manager – Ken Blanchard
Ready to be a Thought Leader- Denise Brosseau
The 21 Irrefutable Laws of Leadership – John C. Maxwell
Facing Leviathan – Mark Sayers
Influencer: The Science of Leading Change – Grenny, Patterson, Maxfield, McMillan, Switzler

5   LEADERSHIP FUNDAMENTALS

Learning Objectives

1. What are the basics that a manager needs to provide.
2. How to build a team culture.
3. What is transformational leadership.

We have all seen the perennial new management "flavor of the month" every year or so. However, despite the onslaught of trendy new management styles, the basic elements of management and leadership have not changed. A return to the basic leadership fundamentals is essential.

"Management is doing things right; leadership is doing the right things." Peter Drucker

What "Management" Provides

Managers not only provide a conduit between the larger enterprise and their teams, but they also contribute four important deliverables:

1. Plan: Outline the scope of work, determine specific goals, create workflows, and generate plans for action. .
2. Organize: Ensure people, equipment, and knowledge are in place. Certify that detailed work is completed correctly and quality is achieved.

3. Coordinate: Create a structure to accomplish, track, and assess goals.
4. Build Culture & Vision: Set the tone and establish vision. This deliverable is the hardest to define and most difficult to teach.

Building Culture & Vision

The manager has the responsibility to demonstrate and reinforce the cultural values the organization desires to instill. Whatever the cultural values are, they must support the fundamental needs all humans share.

Leadership must engender a culture that values and fosters both team and individual growth. There is no single right way to accomplish this, but management must address the basic needs all people share.

Basic Needs

1. Inform: Everyone wants to be in the loop. Part of leading is to keep the troops informed. No one wants to be surprised. This builds trust and respect. It is imperative that everyone understand not only the mission but also the underlying values.

2. Listen: Everyone wants to be listened to and heard. Effective leaders schedule one-on-one meetings, individual lunches and routine meetings among peer groups. Building an effective reporting system reinforces the value of every employee. In order to be effective, a reciprocal reporting system must be actively embraced and supported by the highest

levels of the organization from the line supervisor to the CEO.

3. Contribute: Everyone needs to know that their input is valued and is integrated into the culture.

4. Acknowledge: Everyone needs and deserves recognition.

5. Coach: Everyone benefits from mentoring and coaching. Individuals may not actively seek coaching, but the value of effective mentoring is incalculable.

6. Inspire: Everyone knows inspiration when they see it. The leader may not necessarily be charismatic, but they should create a culture that where enthusiasm and inspiration are possible. Everyone should be able to feel that their work is about more than just a paycheck.

Teams who are informed, heard, and acknowledged for their contributions develop a sense of community and belonging. Effective managers work to deliver these six items, creating and fostering an environment where every employee is valued.

Transformational Leadership - Pulling It Together

The magic of effective leadership is to provide all four Deliverables – Plan, Organize, Coordinate, and Build – while being mindful and engaged in each of the six needs of the team members – inform, hear, contribute, acknowledge, coach, inspire. This is exactly what Transformational Leadership establishes. Transformational leadership is a framework which engenders charisma. When transformational leadership is working, charisma is apparent.

There are four elements to transformational leadership:

1. Influence is the leader's ability to be a positive role model for followers. The transformational leader "walks the talk," and is on the front line working. Transformational leaders make the same sacrifices as their followers. The leader often serves as the "face" of the company and by representing the values his team members embrace, he/she reinforces a connection to the team culture.

2. Inspiration is the ability to motivate followers to perform at high levels and to be committed to the organization or the cause. Inspired employees benefit from company successes because they feel they are an integral part of the organization. The company successes are their successes.

3. Stimulation is challenging followers to be intellectually creative. Employees who are invited to think creatively often contribute solutions to old problems that have defied resolution.

4. Consideration is being responsive to the feelings and needs of employees – as a primary goal. Showing consideration to all employees aligns with the notion of servant leadership.

There is no shortage of resources on leadership and management theories, skills, and techniques. Effective managers acquaint themselves with a variety of theories and points of view. The list below will introduce you to some of the more popular theories.

Takeaways

- ✓ Traditional Managers Plan, Organize, Coordinate, and Build Culture
- ✓ Transformational leaders "walk the walk" and inspire the teams they lead, they stimulate, and consider the emotional state of the team

Exercises

1. Write your own "basic needs" in your own words and views.
2. Come up with 3 or 4 actions that that are things you can do to support those needs.
3. When this is written out, discuss it with your team.

Further Reading

Emotional Intelligence 2.0 by Travis Bradberry & Jean Greaves
Good to Great: Why Some Companies Make the Leap...And Others Don't by Jim Collins
The 21 Irrefutable Laws of Leadership by John C. Maxwell
The 5 Levels of Leadership: Proven Steps to Maximize Your Potential by John C. Maxwell
The Fifth Discipline: The Art & Practice of The Learning Organization by Peter M. Senge

6 GOALS AND MOTIVATION

"The best way to predict the future is to create it." – Peter Drucker

Learning Objectives

1. How to use SMART to set good goals.
2. Understanding motivation.
3. Common mistakes made in goal setting.

Goals

Goals are desired results that you commit to achieving. These can be personal, family, career, organizational, or a combination. Goal setting includes establishing specific objectives with defined completion times. You can have short and long term goals, sub goals, and milestones.

Learn SMART

The SMART concept is attributed to Peter Drucker's management by objectives concept. The mnemonic device SMART stands for Specific – Measurable –Achievable – Relevant – Time.

SMART goal setting is applicable for personal and professional goals. For example a goal of "improve my health" is difficult to define and measure. Improving my health is a vague, non-specific goal that can be an outcome from a dozen or more activities or life changes.

The first step in applying the SMART principle to improving my health is setting a specific goal: reduce my body weight to X pounds and lower my blood pressure to 110/80 – Specific and Measurable. I can directly measure and define the desired end state.

Setting my weight loss target at my ideal weight – that recommended by my doctor – at 165 pounds is desirable, but not Achievable. In order to achieve my goal, it must be something I can actually reach. I would rather set a goal I can actually meet that is a balance between challenge, risk, and the probability of success.

The goal must also be Relevant. If my blood pressure and weight are good, there is no motivation for me to reduce them. Motivation can be sustained if the goal is relevant; otherwise, I will lose interest.

In order to achieve any realistic goal, your goal should have a specific time frame and target date. Even if the goals you've set are short-term goals that are part of a larger project, it is wise to set a Time table that identifies and end point. Sometimes we have multiple goals and milestones that lead up to a bigger goal, but they all have a timeframe for completion. The main advantage of SMART objectives is that they are easier to understand, to track, and see when they are completed.

"Of course motivation is not permanent. But then, neither is bathing; but it is something you should do on a regular basis." - Zig Ziglar

Motivation

Motivation is the desire or willingness to do something, drive, ambition. Motivation is the driving force behind setting and attaining goals. Motivation is the emergent energy that pushes you towards a goal. Motivation is not an innate trait like height – it is a learned skill. Just as there is a method, techniques, and training that can make you a better golfer there are practices, exercises, and behaviors that can boost your personal motivation.

Most of us are motivated by a number of goals. Most individuals are motivated by what our culture says must be done – I need to pay my mortgage so my family has a place to live. I need to save money to send my son to college because I want him to have a successful life. Society embeds this kind of motivation in us. We want to be good citizens and good providers. We are also motivated to do things for personal satisfaction, interest, fun, or challenge. People write books because they are motivated to share a special knowledge or ideas. People who climb mountains do so because of the exhilaration of the challenge. Others volunteer and work long hours for community organizations because they believe that helping others is important. Some individuals are driven to certain tasks because they feel an obligation to do so. Some of us support family members, donate to charities, or volunteer at homeless shelters and soup kitchens because they feel duty-bound. There is clearly a range of motivating factors: have to, want to, obligated to. Understanding what motivates you improves your chances of achieving satisfaction.

Managers and their team members all do better work when we're doing something we like.

Reflecting and understanding you motivations will help reach your desired results. Confirm what you really want. Writing it down in detail can help you confirm this.

Reflecting on your goals and motivations for working toward them will help solidify them. Rethinking where you want to end us may lead to changing your mind. Changing your mind early in the game is not too costly. You've not invested a lot of time, resources, and money. Changing your mind a decade later is a different story. Let's be clear – many people do change careers after investing a decade or two. Marriages and families often reconfigure when partners choose different pathways. It is possible to start over and be successful.

Regardless of where the reflection leads you, the outcomes can be positive with the right motivation. High motivation is key in the completion of long complex tasks that maybe difficult and long, often with limited feedback along the way. Use the steps and the tips below to increase your own level of motivation and help you build up some momentum towards your goals.

"Poor planning on your part does not necessitate an emergency on mine." - Bob Carter

Cost of Misguided Goals and Motivations

When we pursue goals without clearly understanding our personal motivations, we put ourselves, our families and companies at risk. Analysis of our motivations in greater depth results in better outcomes. We might have happier careers, lower job turnover, lower divorce rates, and more satisfying life choices. The examples below are commonplace.

The college student who majors in a particular course of study because she feel she is obligated to follow in the footsteps of an older sibling or parent. After paying tuition for four years studying something for which she has no passion, she realizes another she has no interest in her major. Instead of loving her work in accounting or economics, she discovers that her passion is nursing – it is something that is rewarding and something that she is good at. In the US 80% of college students will change their major during their first year and 50% will make three changes before graduating.

Similarly, the son who begins working in the family restaurant as a teenager and who assumes managing duties as his father gradually retires from the business wakes up one day with nothing but a burning desire to become an engineer. He realizes that he has no love of the business, and worse, no talent for managing or growing the family restaurant.

Consider the hard work and time a young professional puts into his career in hopes of becoming a manager or leader only to learn he actually has little interest in the job or that the "reward" they hoped for actually lies in other professional areas.

Having analyzed, reviewed, and reflected on their goals and motivation can save time, money, and energy. Choosing wisely early on reduces the disappointment and misdirection.

"When defeat comes, accept it as a signal that your plans are not sound, rebuild those plans, and set sail once more toward your coveted goal." - Napoleon Hill

Tips for Goal Setting and Motivation

1. Create your plan. Define your goals. Identify your motivation. Be specific and descriptive. It isn't a plan until it's written down.
2. Use the SMART method.
3. Work the plan. Don't let the plan work you. Be willing to change your mind. Throw out the plan. Change the plan.
4. Classify your motivation: Have to? Want to? Obligated to?
5. Develop achievable, realistic milestones.
6. Incorporate a reward system to mark milestones.
7. Track your progress based on process and not on results. If I want to control my cholesterol by exercising, I can track my results of quarterly blood tests, or I could track the process of how many mornings a week I exercise. I will have 120 times more frequent feedback if I track the process of exercising daily rather than waiting for the result from the quarterly blood work.
8. Develop mental toughness. Everyone experiences setbacks. Stay on track.
9. Become a lifelong learner. The more you know the better you will be able to cope with challenges.
10. Adopt a mindset of improvement rather than achievement. Life isn't pass or fail. Aim for better than yesterday.

11. Mentor others. Helping someone else deal with his challenges may provide unexpected answers to your own challenges.
12. Build a circle of supportive friends, co-workers, and like-minded individuals. Everyone benefits from a supportive web.
13. Evaluate the progress of your plan regularly. Set a monthly meeting with yourself. Adjust or change as needed.
14. Take setbacks in stride. Laugh when you can.

Motivation Myths

We are motivated by money. Although many individuals are interested in becoming wealthy, this myth is basically not true. People are motivated by the absence of what they need. Often this absence is caused by a shortfall of cash. In 1943, Abraham Maslow identified a hierarchy of human needs. He titled his work "A Theory of Human Motivation." In this seminal work on human motivation, Maslow explains the basic needs that motivate human behavior and accomplishment. Once those basic needs are met and people reach a comfortable life style, income itself begins to not be such a relevant factor. One of the strongest motivations driving people is the desire to find purpose. As Maslow theorizes, finding purpose is often not realized until all the basic life needs have been satisfied.

We just lack motivation. Individuals who have not yet found their passion may feel unmotivated. Each individual has to find where his passion lies. Skill and hard work are part of the solution, but no one motivates themselves into defying gravity. Skill and hard work have their limitations. Be honest with yourself, your goals, and what is realistic for you.

Follow your dreams later. Young people are often told to defer the dreams until they are stable. Postponing pursuit of goals is more likely to derail you than trying and failing. If you have a dream and have the passion today, pursue it. You might not have that tomorrow.

I need that motivation book or and seminar before I can really get started. Preparation and ground work can help speed up the process. However, don't look for a magic bean to get the beanstalk growing. Plant the seed yourself. The spark must come from you. No nice and neat cookbook approach will "unlock your true potential."

Everyone is different, so a tool or method that works for Ted might not work for Fred. Basically it's a little inspiration and a lot of hard work.

Six Goal Setting Errors

1. Thinking too big and setting unreachable targets is a sure way to sabotage your plan. Use your imagination and ambition. Once you have developed a goal, make sure it is realistic. Can it be done in the time available with the resources that you control? Use the SMART method to check out your goals when you can.

2. Thinking Pass or Fail during goal setting often results in losing momentum. Life is not a pass or fail proposition. Your goals should not be either. This way of thinking creates an environment of "I am not

good now." The environment should be always "I want to become better." Use SMART goals to establish the trajectory of growth and "bettering" rather than a pass/fail aimed solely at completing a single task. Focusing on growth rather than pass/fail fosters happy intermediate learning outcomes rather than great accomplishments that may result in falling short or failing.

3. Thinking too narrowly as you develop your goals or focusing on an area too small can sabotage your success. Include more areas of your life, career, or work in order to become wider and better rather than narrower and better. Aim to learn one completely new skill a year. Many people focus solely on their career when they set goals. When you set your goals, make sure that you strike the right balance. Although maintaining life balance is different for everyone, it is critical to allocate time and effort to personal as well as professional goals.

4. Thinking too broadly and having too wide of a focus when you define your goals can also sabotage your success. It is a natural tendency to set broad goals in all areas of life. However, most people's resources of time, energy, and money are limited. The focus needs to be wide enough to add solid value and narrow enough to ensure that you have applied the needed depth and rigor within each goal.

5. Not Considering Time Correctly. Underestimating the time necessary to achieve your goals can cause you

to fall short. Pad your timelines a little and consider cutting out other activities if they are not actually part of or supportive to your goals. If you do not estimate duration and completion times accurately, it can be discouraging. Projects that take longer to complete can earn you a bad reputation even if the work is excellent and a later target would have been acceptable had it been put into the plan that way. I like to factor the time I need up by 4-5 fold. Yes, I said 500%.

6. Not Incorporating Systems thinking into your goal setting. Recall the discussion of setting milestones. Completing milestones will ensure you track process, not results. Think in terms of operating a system instead of hitting a target. Track the growth and daily activity of the new system. If your goal is writing a book, a good SMART goal might be to write 5,000 words every day instead of tracking the number of books completed per year. This is a superior method for a number of reasons: it forces you towards leading indicators; it makes your "metric" closer to where the work actually is (gemba), it provides feedback in the workflow rather than at the end, and it allows near real-time adjustment of your work plan. Think process and not results – results will come.

"By working faithfully eight hours a day you may eventually get to be boss and work twelve hours a day." – Robert Frost

Top achievers in every field set detailed goals and use professional coaches to stay motivated and focused. Setting goals provides a clear, long-term vision of the future and at the same time bolsters your daily motivation. It can focus your growth and development, balance your life between work and home, and help organize your time and resources.

Takeaways

- ✓ Use SMART
- ✓ Write down your goals
- ✓ Be realistic about time need
- ✓ Think process and improvement rather than achievement
- ✓ Life is not pass or fail

Activities:

1. Read about Harada Method.
2. Write out 20 things you want to accomplish.
3. What is your motivation for each goal?
4. When would you like to complete each?
5. Before the age of 30
6. In your life
7. In _____ (year)
8. Develop sub-steps for each (a, b, c).
9. Build your goals into a table.

Goal	Motivation	By When	Sub-Steps

7 INTRODUCTION TO CONTINUOUS IMPROVEMENT

Learning Objectives:

1. Process Improvement Methodologies
2. Learn some Assumptions and Principles
3. Become familiar with the Toyota Principals
4. Learn The Waste Types
5. Introduction to a few basic tools

"An organization's ability to learn, and translate that learning into action rapidly, is the ultimate competitive advantage."
Jack Welch

Introduction to Continuous Improvement

There is no segment of industry or business that has not been touched by some aspect of continuous improvement. There are many different traditions and methodologies of continuous improvement, each bringing a slightly different perspective to the concept.

All the process improvement approaches share a few common beliefs:

i) Processes can always be improved;
ii) Measurement and statistics are key to improvement;
iii) Workers nearest the work have the greatest power to improve it.

Most importantly, they stress respect for the individual.

Most of the methods take from or build upon other methodologies freely. A combination of all of these systems has resulted in a set of best practices and practical tools. The better you and your team become at using some of these practical tools, the better. In my experience, a hybrid of these traditions, principles, and techniques creates the most effective workforce.

What Is Continuous Process Improvement?

Process Improvement is the task of identifying, analyzing, and improving upon existing work methods or processes. This is done to reduce waste and achieve a higher level of optimization or quality. It usually involves a systematic problem-solving approach. Each approach brings its own methods, tools, and perspectives to the process. No one approach is better than another. They are simply different schools of thought.

The "Lean" approach is what you might think it is, a management style that emphasizes no excess, no fat, no waste, just enough. The Toyota Company was the first company to embrace Lean management principles. The practice has become so successful in refining processes that it has now become the buzzword in the manufacturing industry. Lean management has five principles, which can be seen in not just manufacturing but in other industries as well. Lean emphasizes removing waste in company resources that are consumed by unnecessary procedures that companies can do without. Lean management introduces seemingly miniscule changes that significantly influence all stakeholders.

It Starts With Culture

Before you can move yourself, your team, or your organization into a process improvement mindset there are a few things you need to come to grips with. In order to adopt a path of process improvement, it is vital that you are aligned with each of these principals.

These principals are fairly common. If you do not ever study any of the actual methods and philosophies at least consider the following:

- You and your teams must believe that they can effect significant change and that you want them to. They need to know they have the authority to make changes and the ability to be successful at it. Remind them daily.

- Focus on the long win - not the short game.

- Implement changes because they are the right changes and can be sustained. Do not anticipate immediate return. If there is a change, it should be done because it is the best choice. It may not have a dollar savings or a clear waste reduction, but do it anyway.

Success: What Is It?

1. Ensure that everyone at all levels understands the values, the mission, how it is tracked and how their individual work connects to the overall goal.
2. Respect and develop people.
3. Teach methodology and tools to everyone. Shop floor consensus is best if not required.
4. Remember that the right process will produce the right results.
5. Accept failure. It is the key step in learning for both individuals and organizations.
6. Build a team of solid players. Discourage superheroes or cowboys.
7. Add value to the organization by adding value to your people. Invest your time, your training, and your patience.
8. Seek information from first-hand sources.
9. Emphasize that process improvement is for everyone. It needs to be owned and used at all levels from the shop floor to the boardroom.
10. Examine your own work and the systems that have always been in place.
11. Identify and remedy waste as the cornerstone behavior of your organization.
12. Implement these changes and reward positive change.

"The most dangerous kind of waste is the waste we do not recognize." - Shigeo Shingo

The emphasis of continuous improvement is to produce incremental improvement without capital expense, upheaval, major retraining, or retooling. Adopt, reward, and promote this skill set. Base changes on frequent, small improvements rather than radical modifications. Infusing the newest technology or expending capital expenses is not what continuous improvement is about.

The focus must be a return to fundamentals that embraces getting as close to the work and the people as possible. There is no assurance that new software, new equipment, or some other trend will have a positive effect on production.

When ideas and recommendation for change come from the workers themselves, the changes are less likely to be dramatically different, and therefore easier to implement. Small improvements are less likely to require major capital investment than major process changes. The ideas come from the talents of the existing workforce, as opposed to the more expensive alternatives of research, consultants, or equipment upgrades.

Implementation of Continuous Improvement

1. Encourage all employees to continually improve their own performance.
2. Encourage workers to take ownership of their work.
3. Reinforce teamwork and collaboration, strategies, which improve worker motivation.

4. Before you move forward, carefully analyze any prospective changes.
5. Define your product or service value from the customer's perspective.
6. Identify the Value Stream.
7. State and draw clearly what the company is doing to create value. You obtain X and convert it using Y in order to produce Z.
8. Observe the process flow and identify any bottlenecks. Be as close to the work as possible.
9. Seek improvement in small steps that can be achieved and sustained.
10. Do not let perfection stand in the way of progress.
11. Analyze the root cause of both successes and failures.
12. Respect everyone. People are the company's real value.

Tips to Ensure Continuous Improvement Is a Success

1. Train yourself and your team. It takes time to adapt to the mindset and philosophy of change. It takes time to learn, demonstrate and internalize the tools.
2. Find an experienced personal guide. Developing the process in-house is more effective than contracting it from an outside vendor. Growing your own internal talent ensures that your team is committed to the project, the team, and the company.
3. Create timelines and milestones. A roll out can take at least a year.
4. Identify key processes and focus on them.
5. Break down key processes into its basic steps.

6. Grow the process by focusing on the process itself, procedures, and tools.
7. Identify how a key action will affect existing processes.
8. Develop a plan to ensure a successful outcome.
9. Determine how to measure success in advance of implementation.
10. Create a process or project mandate which describes the expected outcome, the scope and sequence of the work, and the measurements.
11. Establish timelines and target dates.
12. Identify key elements for each action item.
13. Make specific assignments by name and date.
14. Ensure that accountability is clear, written, and visible.
15. Establish a communication system and use it every time.

"If you can't describe what you are doing as a process, you don't know what you're doing."
- W. Edwards Deming

Brainstorming

Brainstorming combines a relaxed, informal approach to problem-solving with lateral thinking. It encourages people to spontaneously come up with ideas. All ideas are encouraged. Some may be unorthodox or unrelated to the task. Some of these ideas can be crafted into original creative solutions. Other ideas will spark even more ideas.

Brainstorming breaks people out of their comfortable paradigms.

"The world we have created is a product of our thinking; it cannot be changed without changing our thinking." - Albert Einstein

Defer judgment – just catch the ideas. Participants will feel free to generate unusual ideas. Welcome wild ideas. It will yield a long list of ideas – good and not-so-good. They can be generated by encouraging new perspectives and suspending assumptions. These new ways of thinking can give you better solutions.

Brainstorming is a skill that requires practice and coaching. During the brainstorming session, be respectful of everyone. Let each person provide input one at a time. Rank and position do not matter in the brainstorming. Every idea is equal. No one speaks over anyone. No criticism is allowed. Focus on inviting participants to focus on extending or adding to ideas.

Invite participation from everyone. The greater the number of ideas generated, the greater the chance of producing a radical and effective solution. A dynamic brainstorming session where everyone contributes reduces inhibitions, stimulates ideas, and increases overall creativity.

"Efficiency is doing things right; effectiveness is doing the right things." - Peter Drucker

Understanding Waste

1. Movement. Each time material is moved, it requires energy and resources, it risks damage, and it is a cost

for no benefit. Transport does not contribute to the product that the consumer is willingly buying. Reduce movement. Spaghetti diagrams and MIFA (material and information flow) are great tools for reducing this kind of waste.

2. Inventory. Raw materials, work-in-progress, or finished goods represent a cost outlay that has not yet produced an income. Anything in these three silos does not add value and is a waste.

3. Waiting. Whenever products are not in transport or being processed, they are waiting. In traditional processes, a large part of an individual product's life is spent waiting to be worked on, waiting to be shipped, and waiting to be completed. The longer a product languishes, the more the waste. Value stream and process flow mapping are great tools for this.

4. Over-processing. Any time more work than is required is done on a piece, the cost of the piece increases. This may include using tools or materials that are more precise, higher quality, or more expensive than required.

5. Over-production. When more products are produced than are required by your customers, the excess amounts to waste. One common practice that leads to this is the production of large batches. Overproduction is the most dangerous type of waste since it hides all the other waste types. Overproduction leads too much inventory - which requires storage and is prone to decay and spoilage.

6. Defects. Defective products require reworking, rescheduling, replacing, and more frequent checking. This results in more labor costs, more time spent, and more work in progress.

7. Under-leveraged talent. This is the waste associated with under-utilized talent. The shop floor worker who does only his assigned job even though he can bring greater value through his understanding of the work process, the machine, and the defects is not utilized to his capacity. Every employee has other skills - it is wasteful not to take advantage of every skill. Capitalize on the skills and creativity of every employee without regard for their title or tenure or position.

FIVE (5) Why

When you intuit that there is unintentional and unidentified waste, get as close to the problem as you can and see it for yourself. This means that remedying waste at this level requires an in-depth understanding of the processes on the shop floor. This is most effective when the answers come from people who have hands-on experience. When a problem occurs, uncover its nature and source by asking why no fewer than five times.

The 5 Whys is a simple tool that enables you to drill down to the root cause of the problem or cause of waste. When a problem arises, simply keep asking the question why? Continue to ask until you reach the source of the problem and until a clear counter-measure organically emerges

Problem: Your customer is refusing to pay for the material produced for them.

Why? The delivery was late, so the material could not be used.
Why? The job took longer than we anticipated.
Why? We ran out of raw material.
Why? The raw material was all used up on a big, last-minute order.
Why? We did not have enough in feed stock, and we could not order it in quickly enough.

For a more complex or critical problem, use a cause and effect analysis or a more complex tool that might be more effective. This technique can often direct you to the root of the problem. The simplicity of this tool gives it flexibility. It is often a good first step in solving a more complex issue.

Build Your Team's Tool Box

Understanding waste and asking why are the basic tools that build on foundational beliefs. There are literally hundreds of tools and methodologies that have been developed over time. Here are a few of them in short. Learn them each well, one at a time. As your team masters each of them, gradually add one more. Do this forever. When possible, have a skilled practitioner review your work frequently and ensure the tools and methods are being applied well.

1. Single Minute Exchange of Dies (SMED) is one of the many lean production methods for reducing waste in

a manufacturing process. It provides a rapid and efficient way of converting a manufacturing process from running the current product to running the next product.

2. 5S is the name of a method that uses a list of five words – sort, set, shine, standard, sustain. This helps organize the workspace for efficiency by identifying and storing the items used, maintaining the area and items, and sustaining the new order. This usually comes from a dialogue about standardization, which builds understanding among employees of how they should do the work.

3. Poka-Yoke is any mechanism in a lean manufacturing process that helps an equipment operator avoid mistakes. Its purpose is to eliminate product defects by preventing, correcting, or drawing attention to human errors as they occur. A simple example is lines painted in a parking lot to aid the parking cars.

4. Ishikawa diagrams are product design and quality defect prevention tools used to identify potential factors causing an overall effect. Each cause or reason for imperfection is a source of variation. Causes are usually grouped into major categories to identify these sources of variation. The categories typically include: people, methods, equipment, materials, measurements, and environment.

5. Idea PICK chart (Possible, Implement, Challenge and Kill chart) is a visual tool for organizing ideas. PICK charts are often used after brainstorming sessions to

help an individual or group identify which ideas can be implemented easily and have a high payoff.

6. MIFA - Material and Information Flow Analysis. This is a kind of value stream mapping used to create a structured image of the material and information flow on the shop floor. These can be useful, but can be difficult to facilitate the first few times.

Toyota has one of the strongest and most detailed top to bottom operational cultures that deeply imbeds process improvement and quality management into every aspect of their organization. If I were to study only one approach to improvement by one company, it would be Toyota without any question.

The Toyota Way provides the tools for people to continually improve their work. It is powerful, it works, and it is self-contained. Begin your toolbox with the Toyota Way. It is based on the following four starting tenants:

1. Long-Term Philosophy is how we think – Wins are defined in the long game not short term.
2. The Right Process Will Produce the Right Results – focus on getting the process right.
3. Developing People is how you add value to your company in the long term.
4. Organizational Learning is key and is driven by continuously solving problems at every level by digging to the absolute root cause.

The Toyota Principles

Principle 1. Base your management decisions on a long-term philosophy, even at the expense of short-term financial goals.

Principle 2. Create a continuous process flow to bring problems to the surface. Work processes are redesigned to eliminate waste through the process of continuous improvement. The seven types of are overproduction, waiting (time on hand), transport, over processing, extra inventory, motion, and defects.

Principle 3. Use "pull" systems to avoid overproduction. Pull is a method where a process signals its predecessor that more material is needed. The pull system produces only the required material after the subsequent operation signals a need for it. This process is necessary to reduce overproduction.

Principle 4. Level out the workload. This minimizes waste, prevents over-burdening people and stabilizes production rates.

Principle 5. Build a culture of stopping to fix problems to ensure that quality is right the first time. Any employee in the Toyota Production System has the authority to stop the process to signal a quality issue.

Principle 6. Standardize tasks and processes. Standardization is the foundation for continuous improvement and employee empowerment.

Principle 7. Use visual control so no problems are hidden.

Principle 8. Use only reliable, thoroughly tested technology that serves people and processes.

Principle 9. Grow leaders who thoroughly understand the work, live the philosophy, and teach it to others. Leading is teaching.

Principle 10. Develop exceptional people and outstanding teams who follow your company philosophy. All wins are team wins.

Principle 11. Respect your extended network of partners and suppliers by challenging them and helping them improve.

Principle 12. Be aware are of work going on in your unit. Measure twice; cut once.

Become a learning organization through relentless reflection, self-examination, and continuous improvement.

Takeaways:

- ✓ Process Improvement and Lean Management is not about cost cutting – it is about reducing waste and adding value to product.
- ✓ All the "Flavors of Process Improvement" take slightly different approaches. Each of them has environments where they work best. Any of them can help you. Pick one and go!
- ✓ Put as many tools into the "tool box as you can".
- ✓ Train everyone on your team to the fullest extent you can afford.
- ✓ If you have only the time to learn one model, choose the Toyota Way.

Exercises:

1. What are the key processes in your organization or process?
2. Can you draw out your value streams and identify bottlenecks?
3. Can everyone down to the shop floor employee draw out item #2?
4. Do you know what your customers are saying about your product?
5. What value do your customers place on your product?
6. Is it the same as your values?
7. Is everyone in your organization utilized to the fullest extent possible – without regard to their position or educational background?
8. How are you measuring success today and can everyone see it? How often are they aware of this?

Further Reading:

Lean Thinking by James J. Womack and Daniel T. Jones
Toyota Kata by Mike Rother
The Toyota Way by Jeff Liker
Gemba Kaizen by Masaaki Imai
Developing Lean Leaders at All Levels by George Trachilis

8 PROBLEM-SOLVING BASICS

Learning Objectives

1. Learn some basic problem-solving steps
2. Introduction to decision-making
3. Methods and Tips to improve your skills in both

Introduction:

Before you try to solve a problem, you want to think through the problem carefully. Write down what you believe you are solving. Follow the steps below:

1. Write down a careful description of the problem.

2. Talk to the people closest to the work itself.

3. Write down possible solutions. Rank them.

4. Write down what you can measure to test solutions.

5. Test out your solution with a small test batch before rolling it out on a larger scale.

The ability to understand the larger picture, identify the problem, work through different solutions, and find the best path is what separates the good from the great. Problem-solving and decision-making are closely connected and should be considered together.

Problem-solving is the practice of defining, determining the root cause, identifying solutions, prioritizing the steps, selecting alternatives, and implementing a solution. It is okay to feel stress and pressure. Nevertheless, never let pressure make the decision for you – when you feel stressed out, step away from your work.

Everyone has the capacity to be a problem solver. If you have strong problem-solving skills, you have an edge over other leaders, and being able to solve problems is necessary for advancement.

Problem-Solving

So how should you properly resolve a problem? You will develop your own style and methodology over time. Nevertheless, in the beginning, there are steps that you can take in order to get you started on the right track. Here are those steps:

1. Define victory. What is the outcome you are trying to achieve? Do not focus on the first problem you see. The first problem you see might just be a by-product of a deeper issue. Your first step needs to be defining the outcome you are seeking. Only after you determine where you want to reach, can you ask, "How can I get to there?" At this step, you should be able to write down your definition of victory in a single sentence. If you cannot articulate what you want to achieve in a single sentence, you do not understand the situation well enough.

2. Measure it. Is there a metric that can accurately define what the "victory" looks like? This can help track the progress towards the goal and clearly define exactly how we will know we are getting

"better". It is much easier to have a goal of "I want to be more attractive by losing some weight". The metric you use would be your weight in pounds.

3. Map it out. Can you draw out a simple flow chart or model that explains the process in clear-cut terms? This is a vital first step. Drawing out how the system works often helps drive everyone to agree on the process that may never have been clearly defined or not fully understood across the peer group.

4. Gather information. In order to reach your goals, you must be well informed about the system and all the background information in order to reach the goal. Seek out the information from those nearest the work. It is always better to talk to the people on the shop floor than reading the design books. Both will provide you useful information – but the solution lies nearest the work.

5. Understand Variation. Is there a backlog of data to consider? Does the parameter we are seeking to control or adjust have any obvious periodicity? Determine the natural variation and compare the normal distribution to the targets you are after. Will you be able to graphically see the change you are hoping to reach?

6. List possible solutions or options. Build a table with the pros and cons for each solution, cost, and complexity. Brainstorm each solution with 2-3 people and capture all the advantages and disadvantages for each solution on one table.

7. Decide on a path. The best solutions are the easiest to implement and should have the least risk.

8. Vet the solution with a small group that is nearest the work. They will have some ideas to be sure about what might work and what might not. Make sure they understand it is a pilot and a test. Moreover, that you are listening and working with them so that the solution can be their own.

9. Test the solution on a smaller set. If you want to change the way something is done, figure out a way to test it out on a small scale. Try it at one work station, or for just one day,

10. Messaging and training before making any change is crucial. Plan on having to communicate this four or five times more than you think is needed. Taking the time to communicate repeatedly is worth the result. Be patient and explain it again.

11. Track Results. After a predetermined amount of time, revisit the solution and the results. Should the plan be adjusted? Make a point to check-in every week, month, at whatever interval is most appropriate.

12. Study and learn all the steps to the PDCA cycle. You have completed them already in an informal way so it is time for you to learn the detailed methodology. Learn the basic one first; then you should learn the more advanced methods.

Improving Problem-Solving Skills

Imagine how uncomplicated life will be if we were able to solve easily every single problem that comes our way. Fortunately, problem-solving is a skill that can be learned. The first step is to recognize that you want to become better at this. Develop the right amount of confidence, believe in yourself and trust your judgment.

Here are other ways on how you can develop your problem-solving skills:

1. Read all you can about any subject that interests you. Regularly reading and learning over time will vastly improve your ability to solve problems, recognize patterns, and make connections that others may not.

2. Learn to simplify. When you write something, go back later and cross out all the words you do not need. Remove all the big ones. Keep it simple.

3. Doodle. Learn to draw diagrams out to explain problems. This can be the easiest way to understand how the "system" you are examining actually works. When you draw it, you will see other streams or forces that you might have missed.

4. Find the underlying cause of the problem you wish to solve. Ignore other things that complicate the situation. Sometimes, the solutions are right in front of us, but we are so busy over-analyzing that we overlook them.

5. Play logic puzzles or games. This will allow enhancement of your strategic thinking capabilities.

Strategizing is important in resolving a problem and by playing brain-boosting games, you can improve in that area.

6. Ask questions. You are not expected to know everything, but asking will help you fill in the gaps. This will allow you to gather additional facts to help you create a solution.

7. Play music. When you are pressured to solve a problem, you are more likely fail to come up with a good solution. If you are feeling confused, relax and listen to music. It will create a positive impact on your psychological state and free your brain of negative and unnecessary thoughts.

Analysis paralysis

Analysis paralysis is the trap of over-thinking a situation so that an action is never taken. Hence, the never ending "analyze the problem" never ends, in effect "paralyzing" the outcome. Often a decision is treated as overly complicated with too much detail so that a choice is never made and nothing is actually ever done.

To avoid this trap, try the following:

1. Set a deadline. Determine how long you are willing work on solving this problem.
2. Set a "good enough" goal.
3. Approach problems with an iterative mindset. Make it a little better now and a little better the next time rather than waiting for perfection.

4. Start before you feel 100% ready. If you are 80% ready, start now.

Decision-Making

Decision-making and problem-solving go hand-in-hand. Decision-making is an act of choosing between two or more options. It is an important step in solving a problem. Being impulsive when making decisions will take its toll on your relationships, your career and your business. You need to analyze a situation thoroughly before you make a decision.

Great leaders are good decision-makers. If you are developing your problem-solving skills, you should also develop your decision-making skills. While it is a simplification, decision-making is often the final step in the problem-solving sequence.

Often a team will gather facts and develop a series of possible paths, with the positives and negatives of each defined, and pass the responsibility of choosing the path on to a senior manager. Problem-solving and decision-making are two distinctive processes.

Improve Decision-Making Skills

Consider the implications. Before you choose a solution, consider the implications. Sleep on it; consult with a peer or a mentor. Avoid stressors that affect understanding the solution. A decision made under stress is oftentimes a poor one.

Be objective. Put aside your own emotions and rely on facts. Narrow your options. You may have many options initially;

cull the list down so that you will not be confused in choosing the right one. Weigh the pros and cons in all areas that you can think of. Assemble these in a table where each "solution" is a column.

Before making a decision, think of the advantages and disadvantages of the possible result.

Ask for help. Sometimes if you are having trouble making a decision, get help from someone whom you know is an expert in the matter. They may have already experienced what you are going through, so it will not hurt to trust their experience. Along the same lines, seek a challenge if you think you have it nailed down. Once you have assembled your "view of the situation", speak with someone who usually disagrees with you. Bouncing your ideas and assumptions off someone who works for you, or in general agrees with you is probably a waste of time. Seek out someone you know who might disagree with your approach. Discuss it with them and inform yourself of a different view.

Key Takeaways

- ✓ Decision-making is an important part of the problem-solving process.
- ✓ Problems are meant to be solved.
- ✓ Developing your problem-solving skills will help you in your day to day life.
- ✓ Being a great problem solver will help you in your career.
- ✓ Sometimes, the solution to a problem is the most obvious one.
- ✓ Use a process to effectively solve a problem.

Exercises

1. What is the most important decision you have made in your life? How did you go about coming up with that decision?
2. What is a decision a previous supervisor made that you felt was reached correctly.
3. Describe an experience where you have faced a problem at work and how did you resolve it. What would you do differently?

Further Reading:

The Fifth Discipline by Peter Senge
Thinking, Fast and Slow by Daniel Kahneman
Blink: The Power of Thinking Without Thinking by Malcolm Gladwell
The Power of Habit by Charles Duhigg
Lean Thinking: Banish Waste and Create Wealth in Your Corporation by James P. Womack

9 LEARNING THE ART OF DELEGATION

"No person will make a great business who wants to do it all himself or get all the credit" – Andrew Carnegie

Learning Objectives:

1. What is delegating?
2. How to Delegate effectively?
3. What to Delegate?
4. To whom should you delegate?
5. What are the "Levels of Delegation"?
6. Delegating as succession planning and performance management.

What is Delegation?

Delegation is the assignment of responsibility for a defined task to a subordinate during a fixed timeframe. Managing delegations and providing the appropriate coaching, is a fundamental leadership skill. The leader delegates assignments and always remains fully accountable for the outcome and the possible aftermath. The subordinate who is delegated to perform a specific task is responsible for completing the task. There is never abdication of responsibility.

A delegated assignment needs to be vetted comprehensively depending upon the scope, depth, and experience of the contributor. The potential for both "too much checking" and "not enough checking" exists. There must be a balance between the two, depending upon the level of delegation.

Appropriate checks and balances empower a subordinate to make decisions and still have the safety net and benefit of your experience and support. These steps are what make delegation assignments such a valuable learning tool. Effective delegation accompanied by coaching builds skill sets and motivates people. This methodology of delegation, review, and coaching is a powerful tool in the professional development and should have a prominent position in succession planning.

"Don't tell people how to do things, tell then what to do and let them surprise you with the results." --General George Patton

Advantages to delegating assignments:

1. Frees up time for the supervisor to accomplish other work. Delegation enables you to manage by exception. This is a powerful time management tool that you can use to work more efficiently with other people.
2. Boosts the confidence of the employee. It provides some real life "I can." Often this can be the jump-start someone needs to break out of the doldrums.
3. Improves subordinate involvement and interest. This builds their ownership and over time creates an internal locus of control.
4. Gives the subordinates a chance to experience part of a higher level position in the organization. They can ask themselves "is it what I might want for my career" or "is it uncomfortable?"

5. Builds skill sets.

Getting Started

Delegating is actually an art that can be learned. The guidelines below will yield good results.

1. Know your tasks. As a manager, you have many activities going on every day. Identify your tasks at the beginning of each week and identify the tasks that your people can learn from. There are tasks that are not critical, easily understandable, and do not require high level skills. If you do have tasks like this, delegate them. An example would be company roll and attendance checking or minutes of the meetings. For the former, check back with whomever you have assigned the task to would be required.

2. Know your people. Identify people's skill sets. A skills inventory is not an effective inventory if it is not updated regularly. Knowing your people means not only from word of mouth but also by observation.

    People may claim to know something for fear of saying "no". Other people fear that saying "no" to a task is a career limiting move. Give everyone a chance to work on a particular task. The field should be level enough that your people will not feel like they have been left out. Rather than assigning John a task he is already good at, give him something challenging. If your staff is struggling with focus on the job, then make him a minute taker. Engaging people and creating opportunities for skill development is the best way for them to improve.

3. Set expectations for intended results. At the onset of a task, identify the objective of the task and communicate this to the assigned person. Is this particular task exploratory? Is there enough room for your staff to find out ways and means without micro-managing him or her? Ask your staff how they want to complete the given task. Are the instructions clear? You should also communicate why you selected them for the task. Always stay positive and let them know that you trust them. They will complete the task because they are good at it and want to solve the problem.

4. Agree on a deadline. Your task may have a critical deadline. Share the deadline. However, set an earlier date to allow yourself time to review their work over to be sure it meets standards. The submission date must come from them, taking into consideration of when you would need the report or whatever they are working on.

5. Observe and check in. Ensure the staff has ample time to learn the ropes on how to complete the project but do not forget to observe as well. For example, after giving the task of rolling out new company policies for your people, you can sit in and observe while they are rolling out the updated policies. You can also catch the questions when your staff was not prepared to answer them. Observe

measurable outcomes. Ask how long it took your staff to complete the task the first time they did it and explore challenges they may have encountered. Help them figure out how to overcome those challenges.

6. Appreciate your people. Say "thank you" when the delegated task is completed. Since the task was one you were supposed to complete on your own, recognize their efforts. Employees feel satisfaction when they know they are doing well at work. They perform better and feel more involved. A pat on the back or a monthly recognition boosts their confidence. Recognizing them in front of their peers helps a lot too. Do not miss any great performers in your team. Look at the numbers and observe. Any leap in number from a negative to a positive performer should be recognized.

7. Provide effective feedback. Delegating responsibility and work does not require your constant presence. The tasks you delegate to your people are a preparation for them to take on bigger and more complicated tasks. Effective delegation and regular feedback is a part of your succession planning. Informed people know what skills can be gained by successfully completing tasks they have been delegated. Advise them about what they need to work on and how they can improve and then assign the same task. If there are improvements, always let them know.

Communicate your feedback cautiously to ensure that your meaning is clear. Repeat this process to teach new skills and push your people's performance higher. Share the workload.

Delegating as a Performance Management

The goal of every leader should be to duplicate themselves. By duplicating yourself, you can better achieve your team's goals. As your team increases in skills and productivity, share the authority as well. Sharing responsibility and authority will give you insight into how their performance impacts the bigger picture. There will also be times when your staff's performance may overshadow yours. This is a positive outcome that reflects well on your leadership.

Make giving credit to your employees a priority. Many disgruntled employees complain of superiors who do not give them credit for work they have done. This often ends with either the employee moving on to work in another company OR staying but not wanting to participate in any additional tasks.

Avoid micro-managing your people when assigning tasks. Once you micro-manage, you have failed in your goal. Employees must explore the "how" in order for them to learn. Communicate to them the importance of all tasks, small and large, and their role in impacting the bigger picture.

Levels of Delegation

There are a few questions that supervisors should always ask themselves. These questions reveal where you can challenge yourself and your thinking. Always look in the mirror.

Often the results of a delegation suffer when the level of authority is misunderstood. Be sure that you understand your own intentions. Do you want your employees to assess and report back, to assess and complete, or somewhere else in the spectrum? It is worth the time to have some discussion with your reports on how where the boundaries of authority and decision-making lie. Clearly define your expectations to avoid confusion. The list below can help you clarify where these boundaries are.

1. Act. You have empowered your employees to decide what needs to be done and to take care of it. They do not have to have your permission before taking action.

2. Act and Report. You want your employees to decide what needs to be done and do it, but you need to be informed of actions and results. They should report back after taking action.

3. Plan and Act. You want or need to be the final decision maker. Your employees should size up the situations and inform you of the plan. They should not, however, proceed without your specific approval. This course of action is actually a way to protect employees from unexpected consequences. Your level of expertise and knowledge will guide action.

4. Plan and Report. You want or need to be involved in the decision-making process. You want your employees to examine the issues and formulate a plan. However, the potential outcomes are

significant enough that you need to provide input into the process. As manager, you will want to push your employees by having them hash out the details and answer your questions before moving forward.

5. Plan the Approach. You want to encourage your employees to see a variety of options and solutions. Empower them to identify the issues, propose a plan and a few alternatives. Invite them to list the pros and cons of each one and recommend one of the paths, providing reasons for or against the alternatives. Employees will learn how to embrace a path that may not be their first choice.

6. Gather Facts and Return. This path encourages employees to research a problem and the potential outcomes and report back for guidance. Once they have provided the relevant information, you may decide to delegate more responsibility.

Ways to Foster Effective Delegation

1. Focus on enhancing the skill sets of the candidates. Use this as an opportunity for coaching and learning.
2. Ensure that assignments provide a challenge, but are never impossible.
3. Consider their existing workload. If we want them to excel with delegation assignments, you may want to cut some back on some of their other work.

Consider delegating some of their usual work to a level lower below them.
4. Sit with the individual and write out all of the activities they are engaged in. Determine where they can be most effective.
5. Provide more training, if relevant. You may have an employee who is solid on technical grounds, but needs help with communication skills or technology. In collaboration with your employee, determine whether there are specific skill gaps that should be addressed with focused training.
6. Reflect on whether or not you are open to the ideas of others. Effective leaders are open to ideas and willing to change their perceptions.
7. Trust your subordinates. Make sure they know you trust them.
8. Prepare yourself for the pain of productive but critical coaching sessions with your reports. Stretch goals are only as valuable a growth tool as the coaching that must follow. Are you providing adequate follow up? Do you enable team members to learn from their mistakes?
9. Prepare yourself to accept results that are at par. This will enable you to focus on the mission critical elements while delegating the less critical. Prepare yourself to accept these same results at par for the experience of building your teams skill set.
10. Assign on three principles: Is the task something they are familiar with but they can improve the outcomes; is the task a critical task; is this a skill set they can gain and use in the future. Use tasks as part

of your succession planning and performance management.

Delegation with follow up coaching can be hard work. Managers often think it would be easier to simply do a task themselves. It can be done quicker and more efficiently; however, delegation is and essential training tools that can provide insights into possible career paths for the candidate. Always be patient, provide the follow up, and be sure employees know you support them.

Key Take Always:

- ✓ Know your tasks and identify them clearly.
- ✓ Know your people and their skill sets.
- ✓ Set expectations of intended results.
- ✓ Appreciate your people.
- ✓ Provide effective feedback, coaching, and use this to inform your training program.
- ✓ Use these assignments to support succession planning and performance management.
- ✓ Make the levels of delegation a clear part of your team's daily language.

Exercises:

1. Prepare a succession planning map – where do you think each person can be in the future?
2. What skills will they need in preparation for those positions?
3. What tasks do you think you can delegate for them to learn those skills?

4.	What is the timeline for your people to gain new skills?

Further Reading:

Work Less, Do More – Jan Yager
How to Delegate – Robert Heller
Don't Do. Delegate! – James M. Jenks

10 SERVANT LEADERSHIP

"The simplest and shortest ethical precept is to be served as little as possible . . . and to serve others as much as possible."
- Leo Tolstoy

Learning Objectives

1. What are the 9 characteristics of Servant Leadership?
2. What does locus of control mean?
3. What does service minded mean?

Understanding "Service"

The servant leadership model holds that a leader's primary role is to serve employees. Service orientation, peer level service orientation, and leader servant orientation are all variations on a theme.

Foundational elements of this theme are as follows:

1. Doing more than required or "Service Mindedness"
2. Believing that you make a difference or Self-efficacy
3. Striving to improve the team and not the leader – "winning for we, not me"

Developing Empathy

Customer service orientation can be defined as going the extra mile to make things right for the customer or "receiver". This may be challenging to understand, but you know when you are receiving it, and when you are not.

Keep in mind that the receiver need not be an actual customer in the traditional sense. It does not need to be a cash-paying customer who receives "goods" in a transactional sense. The "customer" can be another department at work, part of the office, division of your company, or any downstream stakeholder in the value stream. Peer level service orientation is that which occurs when a peer, rather than a leader, steps outside of their normal boundaries and helps in a deeper manner than is normally expected. People with this orientation, or paradigm, "live" in this manner all of the time. They have a sense that their influence and responsibility to team and community is broad and vitally important. Servant-leaders focus primarily on the growth and well-being of their team. They manage, lead, and direct in every traditional sense. Beyond this, they enable their subordinates because their orientation is to provide support - not to control. Servant leaders share power. They do make hard decisions, manage and enforce. When required, they make the unpopular choices. Nevertheless, this is done from a position of service, support, and love.

Providing service to your subordinates, peers, leaders and society goes beyond doing the minimum. It pushes one past doing for me - it is doing for "we".

"A leader is best when people barely know he exists. When his work is done, his aim fulfilled, they will say: we did it ourselves." - Lao Tzu

Servant Leadership

"Servant Leadership" is a management philosophy and a set of leadership practices that sit in stark contrast to traditional management paradigms. Traditional leadership involves the accumulation of power, the ladder to climb, the top of the food chain. You progress upwards to reach the most power.

In contrast, the servant-leader shares power, puts the needs of others first, and helps people develop and perform. These principles make up their core. They are not occasional, sideline principles. Servant leaders are all about the development and mentoring of others. Leadership is providing tools, environment, and "serving."

Servant leaders build relationships, not power structures. They emphasize collaboration, trust, empathy, and relationships. They lead in order to better serve those around them. Their mantra is dialogue over dictate; empathy over enterprise.

A servant-leader focuses primarily on the growth and well-being of people and the communities to which they belong. They provide an enabling environment. Their natural orientation is to provide, not to control. Servant leaders share power with (or empower) their subordinates and peers. They put the needs of others first.

They encourage, support, and enable subordinates to blossom into their full potential. This leads to delegation of responsibility and participative decision-making. They help others develop even if they are outside of the team or even the organization. Below are some servant leader behaviors we should all become self-aware of and work to enhance in ourselves.

"We make a living by what we get. We make a life by what we give." -Winston Churchill

Nine Servant Leader Characteristics

1. Listening. Servant leaders seek to identify and clarify the thoughts of a group; they listen receptively to hear the inner voice of the speaker; they grasp what the spirit and mind are communicating.

2. Empathy. Servant leaders strive to understand and empathize with others. Everyone needs to be accepted. Effective managers assume good intentions of coworkers and do not reject them even when forced to reject their behavior or performance. This does not mean, "I am okay, you're okay." Nor does it mean adopting other people's emotions as your own.

    Embracing empathy is not pleasing everyone. An empathetic leader thoughtfully considers the team's feelings in the process of making intelligent decisions. Valuing the ideas of others, not dictating your choice or preference, is one important factor of an effective leader.

3. Healing. Robert Greenleaf, the father of modern servant leadership, says, "There is something subtle communicated to one who is being served and led if, implicit in the compact between the servant-leader and led is the understanding that the search for wholeness is something that they have."

4. Awareness. General awareness – especially self-awareness – is a strength of the servant-leader. The elements of emotional intelligence should be exercised and developed in servant leaders.

5. Persuasion. Effective leaders rely on persuasion, rather than positional authority in making decisions. Seek to convince others. This is the clearest distinction between the traditional authoritarian leadership and that of servant-leadership. The servant-leader is effective at building consensus within groups. It does not need to be my way - but a way we can all live with that works.

6. Conceptualization. The servant leader does not fear understanding, sharing, and developing mental models of issues being faced. Instead they rely on sharing and building a shared vision across the teams and community.

7. Foresight. Foresight enables leaders to understand lessons from the past, the realities of the "now", and the consequences of a decision in the future. It is a kind of wisdom; it is connected to mental models and shared vision.

8. Stewardship. Leaders play significant roles in holding their institutions in trust for the greater good of society. Treat it like your own - but know you are only taking care of it for a time.

9. Building Community. All effective leaders seek to identify a means for building community among those who work within a given institution and the community at large. This is something they do every day - not a once a year gift to the United Way. It is a lifestyle.

Principals of Servant Leadership

1. The higher one is in the organization, the greater your obligation to serve.
2. Leaders come last, or not at all - never first.
3. Promotions and resources are made in order to serve more - not to be served more.
4. Effective leaders respond to employee complaints with the same urgency used for customers.
5. Leaders empower teams and delegate progressive levels of authority until their job becomes obsolete.
6. Teams, not individuals, own the "wins." Failures are owned by the leader.
7. Conflicts between individual needs and organization needs are made to serve the groups best interest.
8. Servant leaders care about everyone the organization touches even when well outside of the company itself.
9. People are hired, trained, empowered, and coached in order to for them to succeed.
10. The imperatives of leadership are development of subordinates, transparent communication,

engagement, and shared vision. All business goals are secondary to these.

Locus of Control & Self Efficacy

Locus of control refers to the extent to which individuals believe they can control events affecting them. The concept was coined and developed by Julian Rotter in the 50's and has since become an aspect of personality studies. There are two types of locus of control - internal and external. Internal locus of control is the belief that you are "in charge of the events that occur." External locus of control is the belief that "chance, fate, or other forces determine events."

Individuals with an internal locus of control believe their behaviors are directed by their personal decisions and efforts. They have control over those things they can change. They live in the "I" space. Having an internal locus of control is linked to self-efficacy, the belief that you have the ability to do be successful at a task or in life.

People with an external locus of control see their behaviors and lives as being controlled or driven by fate. They are stuck and their belief makes it true. They live in the "victim" space. They view themselves as victims of bad luck, fate, or circumstance. They may believe they are prohibited from success.

Individuals with a strong internal locus of control believe events in their life emerge and develop primarily from their own actions. For example, when receiving test results, people with an internal locus of control tend to praise or blame themselves and their abilities. People with a strong external locus of control tend to praise or blame external factors such as the teacher or the test.

Self-efficacy is a person's belief that he or she can accomplish a particular activity. It differs from locus of control by relating to competence in situations and activities. Self-efficacy plays an important role in one's career because when people feel that they have self-efficacy over their work conditions, the environment becomes less stressful. Believing they have the capacity to complete a task enables them to focus on the work and not "run scared." Training in coping skills, team dynamics, and the change grief process increases self-efficacy and internalizes locus of control.

"The miracle is this--the more we share, the more we have."
-Leonard Nimoy

Being Service Minded and "The Extra Mile"

Service-minded leaders believe they are accountable for their work and personal life. Instead of asking who is to blame for a situation, a service-minded individual asks "What can I do to improve the situation? They say this because they believe they can change it – and they want to.

For this paradigm to work, a number of skills are essential:

- ability to accept change
- attentiveness
- calmness
- communication
- emotional intelligence
- focus
- high personal accountability

- knowing THEY CAN
- optimism
- patience
- risk taking
- willingness to learn

Going the "extra mile" is characterized by the individual who does more than the minimum required and who performs well beyond par in a way that requires them to step outside of their normal duty to provide greater support with an attitude of generosity. This might be something that actually is not easy for them and may even expose them to risk or criticism where performing their normal function would not expose them to this liability. They give of themselves in a way to lift up the "other" – not for reward or personal gain. They demonstrate this service without expecting anything in return.

Working for the "We"

Servant leadership is a "transformational" leadership model. This paradigm is punctuated by a leader that empowers, challenges employees to identify change, leads through inspiration, and operates through influence. They do this by empowering their teams and organizations to do this for themselves rather than being dragged along. Transformational leaders rely very little on authority. Their sphere of influence is much wider than their organizational reporting structure. They provide a higher level of organizational vison than the traditional leader.

This model is in contrast to the more traditional "transactional" model, which is based on a "give and take" relationship: employees perform work and receive reward, reach a stretch goal –receive a bigger reward. In the transactional model, all influence is within the normal reporting umbrella; rules and structure are taken as absolute; the worldview is static.

Mutual Empathy

Followers of servant leaders typically feel deep trust and respect for the leader. Because of this, they work harder than expected and grow beyond normal expectations. This occurs because the leader offers something more. More than working for pay, they provide followers with an inspiring mission. They share the vision and allow them to co-create their own unique identity.

Servant leaders support the individual. Leaders demonstrate genuine concern for the needs and feelings of followers. Personal attention to each follower is a key element that brings out his or her best. The team wins by striving to help every team member along. The leader does not build them up but instead diminishes himself while at the same time promoting the accomplishments and needs of the individual.

The leader does each little step right with each individual. Servant leaders offer intellectual stimulation and challenges followers to be innovative and creative. They force their team members to break out of their comfort zones and become engaged on the next deeper level. They move the groups to greater abstract understanding while at the same time challenging them on what is achievable when the "status quo" model is discarded.

Takeaways

- ✓ Servant leaders lift their teams up
- ✓ Nine Servant Leader Characteristics
- ✓ Empathy is a vital characteristic of a leader
- ✓ Why is it important to have a central locus of control

Exercises

1. Identify a few of the best leaders you have worked for in your career. For each write out what they did that made them great. Can you emulate these traits in your own leadership?

Further Reading

Greenleaf, Robert K. Servant Leadership: A Journey Into the Nature of Legitimate Power and Greatness
Wiseman, Liz. Multipliers: How the Best Leaders Make Everyone Smarter
Miller, John G. QBQ! The Question Behind the Question: Practicing Personal Accountability at Work and in Life
Maxwell, John. Developing the Leaders Around You: How to Help Others Reach Their Full Potential

11 COMMUNICATION: HABITS, BEHAVIORS, AND EXPECTATIONS

Learning Objectives:

1. What is your communication preference?
2. What is a communication faux pas that your team has agreed not to do?

Communication is at the core of every human endeavor and perhaps the defining element of humanity itself.

Wikipedia says communication "is a purposeful activity of exchanging information and meaning across space and time using various technical or natural means, whichever is available or preferred. Communication requires a sender, a message, a medium and a recipient, although the receiver does not have to be present or aware of the sender's intent to communicate at the time of communication; thus communication can occur across vast distances in time and space. Communication requires that the communicating parties share an area of communicative commonality".

Consider this example: Two network engineers are at a gun range sighting in a rifle. One is at the bench firing the rifle. The second is at the target pit pulling targets. After every string of shots, the target pit calls out a miss. After several frustrating attempts, the man at the firing line places his hand over the muzzle and squeezes off one more shot. Gleefully with a hole through his hand he proclaims

"Everything checks out on this side – the problem must be on your end." That is how communication works. One needs to always meet the other farther towards the middle than halfway. When building a new team, the leader should describe and promote positive habits to support better communication.

No matter what our workplace environment looks like, we all apply the following values in managing communication:

1. Face-to-face is the preferred communication method.
2. Phone calls are better than emails.
3. Structured meetings are the best method for communication to groups.
4. Conference calling is a cost effective option where a physical presence is not mandated.
5. If you are using conference calling or virtual presence, make sure your equipment is actually providing a usable platform.
6. Email and meeting notes are not the preferred method of communication.
7. Inflammatory communication has no place in our culture.
8. If you do not want to read it on Facebook or would not speak it to your daughter, do not email it.
9. Sensitive communication should not be made via email.
10. In answering an email, avoid "reply all." It is wasteful and disrespectful of others' time.

11. Relationships are the conduit of communication – build them.
12. Face-to-face meetings requiring travel can be expensive and should be reserved only for the required personnel. This protects both human and economic resources.
13. During meetings, our cultural norm is to silence cell phones.
14. The use of computers, cell phones, iPads, and personal assistant devices is frowned upon during meetings.
15. Routine meetings benefit from visual meeting tools and techniques where possible to improve communication.
16. If there is not dialogue, you are not communicating
17. When meeting with outside entities, be cognizant of company image. You are representing your company and your team.
18. Be on time. If you are not 15 minutes early, you are late.
19. Be properly dressed. Really. Match your job and audience.
20. If your meeting relies on any computer or projection equipment, set it up and test in advance.
21. Do not rely on performance management software or other "aids" to serve as a substitute for face-to-face communication. This is especially true of performance management and training.

22. "Listen and discuss" is preferred to "click and learn."

If you have other behaviors to improve communication please send them to me, or share your experiences with some comments.

Take Aways:

1. Everyone has a preference for how they want to communicate.
2. Email is the least effective method of communication.
3. Reply All should be eliminated.

Exercises

1. Have a brainstorming meeting with your team to discuss how to improve communication.
2. List each of your direct responses and how each prefers to communicate.
3. With your team, draft your own "communication charter."

12 WHY YOU MUST POINT OUT WHAT "GOOD" LOOKS LIKE

Learning Objectives

1. Why we message desired behaviors
2. Some basics about giving praise in front of peers

When building a new team, if you see "good" work, point it out as an example of positive behavior. The acknowledgment and reinforcement of "good" activities is essential. To foster this activity an example helps illustrate the landscape and develop the expectations of the team.

Everyone needs to apply judgment to specific situations and individual preferences. It helps everyone to call out what "good" looks like and what we would like to enhance and built upon in others and in ourselves. It is like kids playing baseball. Coaches call out the moves that are good: nice hit, nice throw, good hustle, good teamwork. Calling out what is good helps all the players.

Incorporate pointing out good work when you see it! Make this a normal aspect of day-to-day practice.

Any one level of the organization should feel comfortable recognizing co-workers for both individual and group achievements. Recognize individuals for both activity and behavior that were successful, and/or behaviors that were admirable. It does not have to be a win - just the right behavior. Reward the behavior and not the result.

It is important for each person to be distinguished for his/her own contribution. Group recognition contributes to team building and informs the group that together, they are valuable to the organization.

To be effective, recognition must be sincere and heartfelt. People sense if their efforts are acknowledged only out of duty or if comments are lacking in sincerity. When you mention something, be sure you mean it.

Acknowledgement of effort and accomplishments must be timely in order to be effective.

Remember that each person has their own preferences for how they want to be recognized - what one appreciates could be a real turn-off for someone else. Managers must always respect the individual.

This should be informal, delivered among peers, and frequent – but it must be delivered. ALL levels must participate in this effort.

Takeaways

- ✓ It is important to demonstrate what is desired
- ✓ Repeating is key to enforcing positive change
- ✓ The best way to teach your team what you expect is to point out daily examples of others who are hitting the mark

Exercises

1. Take a moment tomorrow and thank someone for something they did that was above and beyond. Do this in front of their peers if you can.
2. Do something tomorrow yourself to help out someone to make something better in the office.

Suggested Reading

Ok. This one is going to be a stretch. But if you like sociology and case studies this I s a great read that explains a lot of social contracts and why we are encouraged towards some behaviors and pushed away from others based on our social contract. The individual in a social world, by Stanley Milgram

13 INTRODUCTION TO THE CHANGE CURVE

Learning Objective:

1. What are the stages of the change grief process?

I would wager everyone is already familiar with the Change-Grief process. It has proven valuable to my team to have some group discussions about the Change-Grief process and to become familiar with the ups and downs this phenomenon can cause our group. The "Change Curve" is a useful tool when managing team change.

Understanding where an individual is on the curve will help when deciding how and when to communicate information, what level of support someone requires, and when best to implement changes.

Furnishing individuals with the knowledge that everyone experiences the same emotions is the best way to return to good performance, job satisfaction, and general happiness. It helps boost the individual's self-awareness and the entire teams "team-awareness." It improves our collective emotional intelligence. If you are leading a new team through uncharted territory, reviewing this with them will benefit everyone.

Introduction

The Change Curve is based on a model originally developed in the 1960s by Elisabeth Kubler-Ross to explain the grieving process. Since then it has been used as a method of helping people to understand their reactions to significant change or upheaval.

During a large project, there are many changes and reorganizations that can cause disconnects between how the project develops and what role the individual contributors play – and what roles they are expected to play. This mismatch between practice and expectations often causes a grief/change process.

Kubler-Ross proposes that a terminally ill patient progresses through five stages of grief when informed of their illness. She further proposes that this model can be applied to any dramatic, life-changing situation. By the 1980s; the Change Curve was a firm fixture in change management circles. The curve and its associated emotions can be used to predict how performance is likely to be affected by the announcement and subsequent implementation of a significant change.

The original five steps of grief – denial, anger, bargaining, depression and acceptance – have been adapted over the years. Although there are many versions of the change curve in existence, the majority of them are consistent in their use of the following basic emotions, which are often grouped into three distinct transitional stages.

Stage 1 – Shock & Denial

The first reaction to change is usually shock. This initial shock, while frequently short lived, can result in a temporary slowdown and loss of productivity. Performance tends to dip sharply. Individuals who are normally clear and decisive seek more guidance and reassurance, and agreed-upon deadlines can be missed. The shock is often due to lack of information, fear of the unknown, fear of looking stupid, fear of doing something wrong. After the initial shock has passed, it is common for individuals to experience denial. At this point, focus tends to remain in the past. There is likely to be a feeling that if everything was OK as it was, why must I change?

Individuals who have not previously experienced major change can be particularly affected by this first stage. It is common for people to convince themselves that the change is not actually going to happen, or if it does, that it will not affect them. People carry on as they always have and may deny having received communication about the changes. They may make excuses to avoid taking part in forward planning.

At this stage, communication is key. Reiterating what the actual change is, the effects it may have, and providing as much reassurance as possible will all help to support individuals who are experiencing these feelings.

Stage 2 – Anger & Depression

After the feelings of shock and denial, anger is often the next stage. A scapegoat, in the shape of an organization, group or individual, may become the focus of blame. Focusing the blame on someone or something enables a continuation of the denial by providing another focus for the fears and anxieties the potential impact is causing. Common feelings include suspicion, skepticism, and/or frustration. The lowest point on the curve occurs when the anger begins to wear off and the realization that the change is real hits.

It is common for morale to be low, and for self-doubt and anxiety levels to peak. At this point, performance is low. Many will continue to work in the same way even if this is no longer the right method.

Providing information about the Change Curve helps develop a more stable environment.

Stage 3 – Acceptance & Integration ("Moving On")

After the rough emotions subside, a more optimistic and enthusiastic spirit is born. Individuals accept the change and begin to work with the changes rather than against them. Next come thoughts of new opportunities and also relief from surviving the changes.

The final steps involve integration where the focus is on the future and there is a sense that real progress can be made. By the time everyone reaches this stage, the new situation has replaced the original. It has become the new reality. During the early part of this stage, energy and productivity remain low, but slowly begin to show signs of recovery. People given specific tasks or new responsibilities will have questions.

Communication remains key. Regular progress reports and the recognition of good work will help shore up the now growing positive mood.

We Are All Individuals

Each person reacts individually to change, and not all will experience every phase. Some people may spend a lot of time in Stages 1 and 2, while others who are more accustomed to change may move fairly swiftly into Stage 3.

Generally, people move from Stage 1 through Stage 2 and finally to Stage 3 – but there is no right or wrong sequence. Several people going through the same change at the same time are likely to travel at their own speed and will reach each stage at different times. You can lead your team to work in the status quo - or you can mentor them to embrace change, understand their own emotional dynamic, and evolve through change with the least pain.

Takeaways

- ✓ Everyone goes through the process
- ✓ No one skips step
- ✓ There is no proper speed – everyone is a little different

Exercises

1. What has your biggest change been?
2. How did you cope with it?
3. Draw out your support system?
4. How would you have done the change in question #1 differently?

Further Reading

HBR's 10 Must Reads on Change Management (including featured article "Leading Change," by John P. Kotter), by Harvard Business Review

14 BUILDING A CULTURE OF TEAM ACCOUNTABILITY

Learning Objective:

1. What is accountability?

The most powerful way a leader can create passion is by establishing an effective system of accountability, which measures performance and directs appropriate action. Understanding the pivotal role of accountability in the workplace and using it to drive success and impassion the workers is the key to everything else.

Building a culture of accountability will take time – a new team culture can emerge in as short a time as 4 months. An established team may take far longer.

Begin by establishing clear roles that define both team and individual ownership. People struggle to be accountable when roles are ambiguous. Remove any confusion. Use visual tools whenever possible - people do not internalize information until they visualize and internalize the situation.

Focus on processes. Each member is obliged to seek information, give and receive feedback, and point out the need for corrective action at any time. There must be clear levels of accountability and reporting to specific roles – the supervisors should be accountable to the superintendents who, in turn, are accountable to the unit mangers and so on.

Freedom and Control

Most problems have multiple answers, so give people the free hand they need to make decisions. The first solutions your teams and direct reports come up with will probably be good. Improve upon them instead of inserting your own. Support is the key – be sure people have the resources, knowledge and assistance they need.

Force team members' growth and make assignments with this approach. Team members increase their skills, confidence and ownership.

Reward behavior, judgement, and process over results. Give praise to the right choices and directions. Never punish for failure. Reward those doing the right things and results will follow.

If a team member is not engaging, coach them. Those who are "owning it" and struggling need more coaching, one-on-one time, and hand holding to get started. Those who are not embracing their ownership need to be counseled and if they are not able to change, they must be transferred to a position of better fit. They poison the soup. Remove the poison.

Accountability is the foundation for creating a learning organization. If you want sustainable high-quality processes, you need to be able to see what is working and what is failing. Analyze the cause. Everyone must be able to speak freely, understand together, and discuss openly what aspects of the situation have influenced the outcome. This must come with the free hand to make changes.

Expectation of Evaluation

In accountable organizations, no one expects to "stay under the radar." People seek feedback because they know it is intended to improve the process, build their knowledge, and enhance their careers. Organizations lacking multiple feedback mechanisms only discover shortcomings when it is too late.

Build Integrity

Call people out if they do not complete what they say. When anyone falls short, he/she admits it and works to improve. If someone is consistently falling short, it should be an alarm that something is missing in your culture of accountability.

Takeaways

- ✓ Understanding roles is important
- ✓ Holding peers accountable makes the team stronger

Exercises

1. What are your key responsibilities and deliverables in your current position?
2. Write them down.
3. Do you know the deliverables of each of your peers?
4. How do you know when you are hitting the mark?
5. How do your peers know?

Further Reading

The Fifth Discipline: The Art & Practice of The Learning Organization, by Peter M. Senge

15 TIPS FOR MORE PRODUCTIVE COACHING

"Do. Or do not. There is no try" – Yoda

Learning Objectives

1. One on one coaching is a powerful tool
2. Listen more than you speak
3. Provide empathy

Firefighters run towards the fire – not away from it. Managers and contributors alike should run toward evaluations, feedback, and coaching rather than attempting to "stay under the radar." Personal mastery will not develop without embracing constructive criticism and actively reinventing oneself forever - this is our goal. How much time do you spend with your employees? Think about how much dedicated time each employee receives in direct and focused coaching. Time focused directly on their individual performance and development. In many cases, the individual attention is not on the high end of the scale.

One-on-one coaching is crucial to close this gap. Regular performance reviews, staff, and project review meetings are not frequent enough. They are not focused on the individual or constructively critical enough to be of benefit. One-on-one coaching sessions are opportunities for employees to share their ideas, frustration, and career advancement with their managers in a private setting. It is also another vehicle to keep the individual focused in the right direction AND keep the manager aware of their needs and issues.

Dialogue - not broadcast.

The list below provides useful guidelines for workplace coaching.

1. The key to effective coaching is the understanding that it is employee-focused. Not goal focused.
2. Resist the urge to make it about you and what you want – think "them." The manager's role is to listen and to draw the key issues out of the employee. It is the questions you ask that matter – not the answers they are looking for.
3. Managing should be 90% listening and 10% talking.
4. Managers should use the one-on-ones to ask for feedback on their own performance and suggestions for change. It is a two-way street. You will benefit from this information if you take it to heart and act upon it.
5. The frequency and duration depends on the situation - usually 30 minutes works well every other week. It does depend on the person and the type of issues. There will be some situations where one hour per week is required. Challenged employees, newly formed teams, or special project considerations may influence this.
6. Some managers may find coaching time consuming and will not spend the energy. This is to everyone's detriment. They need to perceive these sessions more as regular "reality checks" to ensure alignment of employees' goals to those of the company. If you are not willing to spend this time with each report, is your position in alignment with your values or personality?

7. Coaching sessions will result in more motivated employees who know they are being recognized for their contributions to the company.
8. Employees will feel that management cares about their ideas and career advancement within the company.
9. A high retention rate of high-performing and motivated employees will save your company money in the end (and it will improve the quality of your day-to-day life right now!)
10. Both employees and managers dread one-on-ones when they know it involves constructive feedback. It pushes us out of our natural comfort zone.
11. Talk about the issue in an objective manner and allow them to share their perspectives.
12. MOVE FORWARD. Do not stall on what they did; focus on what they will do in the future. Encourage them to come up with a plan to remedy the issue. Do not cry over spilt milk.
13. Keep in mind that all employees react differently to constructive feedback.
14. Offer your support in developing a plan only if they are struggling to come up with their own.
15. Finish the discussion by setting a follow-up session to keep track of the employees' progress.
16. Show enthusiasm when they achieve what they have set to do. Leave the session on a positive note.
17. When you have to, look for a win; make a victory when you need to have one.
18. Body language is important in setting the tone for the meeting.

19. Do not separate yourself from the employees by sitting across a conference table. Have an open presence by sitting facing them with arms uncrossed.
20. Be open and receptive to what they have to say.
21. Make eye contact to show them that you are actively listening and that you are genuinely interested in what they are saying.
22. Be respectful and do not look at your phone or watch throughout the session. If you have an important call, set that expectation at the start.
23. Take notes. It is worth your time to develop a worksheet for this purpose. It will help you remember the important points of the conversation and is useful for follow-up sessions. It is also a way to show the employees that you are listening to them.
24. Coaching is not only about giving positive and constructive feedback. It is a chance for line managers to gather suggestions from direct reports on the bigger picture. Ask the employees for their input on where the unit, project, or team is heading. This is an opportunity to ensure that strategic objectives by the leaders of the organization are "lined-up" with the teams' tactical execution.
25. Give reports the opportunity to come up with new ideas and share them with the line manager.
26. They may have better insights on how the organization is doing since they are the primary contact with the work. They are closer to the tools.
27. Ask what they are trying to achieve in support of the company's mission and vision – also be aware and ask about their individual goals and priorities.

28. Knowing where your employees are aiming towards can help you build your succession pipeline.
29. Ask your employees what they think the team as a whole is doing well and what their teams have been struggling to achieve.
30. Recognize them for their achievements and contributions to your overall objectives. You may have missed some positive accomplishments and this is the perfect setting for you to learn them.
31. Encourage employees to provide constructive suggestions for the future.
32. Ask your employees - If you were your own coach, what suggestions would you have for yourself?
33. By listening to their suggestions, you can then modify your own suggestions to better reflect the strategic objectives of the company.
34. Listening to your employees, you can provide the appropriate support to ensure that their suggestions are being implemented effectively.
35. You can also participate by suggesting approaches and asking whether the approach will be helpful to become more effective.
36. Managers need to remember that improvement is not measured by the frequency of one-on-ones, but by the quality of them.
37. The key to improvement is to provide coaching to the right people on the right topic.
38. What suggestions do you have for me? This question makes the one-on-ones a two-way conversation.
39. Managers who ask for feedback and focus on improving the key behaviors are more likely to have an increase in leadership effectiveness. Employees

are more open to the idea of being coached, when their managers are willing to be coached by them.

Becoming an effective coach requires trial and error. There is no perfect formula on how to be the best coach since every company and person is different. The results of effective coaching affect both the managers and employees. For the manager, one-on-ones provide a structure for guidance and focus, which leads to higher productivity. Employees have greater satisfaction as coaching allows them to share their ideas and career plans. Everyone one of us wants to have a voice. If careful notes are taken and retained in a systematic manner this process makes annual reviews much easier and less stressful for everyone.

Coaching takes us all out of our comfort zone. Remember to be courteous, be consistent, be honest, be respectful – but above all else make sure you are listening.

Takeaways

- ✓ Coaching is one of the most important things managers do
- ✓ There is more listening needed and less talking
- ✓ Asking for feedback is important as a leader

Exercises

1. What was the most difficult message you have ever had to receive at work?
2. How was it delivered? How did you respond?

3. How could it have been done better?
4. What is the worst received feedback you have ever had to provide?
5. How could you have done it better?

16 BUILDING TEAM TRUST AND THE SAFE SPACE

Learning Objectives

1. How to establish Trust
2. What is collaboration

Teams & Collaboration

Most work is done by teams composed of peers with a chair or a leader. A team is a collection of people who are working in a common area. They may have different functions or levels, but they are essentially team members. Teams work using a collaborative method. That is a fancy way of saying they share and talk to each other. They build on each other's ideas. They grow and pollinate each other's thinking.

It is that simple - teams share, talk, and build on each other's ideas. This allows them to complete work faster and of better quality than they could functioning alone. Leveraging this synergy allows the sum of the team to be greater than the sum of the individuals.

The lynch pin to this is TRUST - without peer level trust, communication (talking) and collaboration (sharing and building on each other) are lost. When this is lost, the sum of team actually becomes LESS THAN the sum of the individuals. It is actually counterproductive.

Peer Trust

I trust people who keep their word. We tend to like those who say "A" and then actually complete "A". We become uncomfortable working with those who say "A" and then provide "a". We begin to avoid and distrust those who claim "A" was competed but never produce anything. In general, trust blossoms from "Say what you do and do what you say". Many have lost this simple principal.

If someone lets you down a number of times, then you know they are not reliable. This limits your desire to share with them - and it breaks collaboration. Collaboration is the method teams use to work together, so when trust is broken, the power of a team is broken. Relationships thrive on trust. When trust dies, relationships end and productive collaboration stops.

How to Establish and Maintain Peer Trust

Here are some pointers, tips, and thoughts to help build and foster trust and build "trusting relationships"

Listen deeply. Listening is opening yourself up to change. It is not listening when you are waiting for your turn to respond. Think dialogue - dialogue builds trust.

"We have two ears and one tongue so that we would listen more and talk less." –Diogenes

Do what you say. If you cannot deliver, do not promise. Saying it is promising. Your word must be your bond. If you do have to go back on your word, be direct, clear, honest, and apologetic. No double standards. Be equal in your treatment and response to everyone.

Always respect the alternative view. It might be the one you adopt tomorrow or maybe right now. Learn to understand the alternative path.

"You can't see change until you change the way you see."-- Raimy Diaz

"What you do speaks so loud that I cannot hear what you say."-- Ralph Waldo Emerson

Your words become your actions, your actions become your habits, your habits become your values, and your values become your destiny." — Mahatma Gandhi.

The guidelines below will ensure peer trust:

1. Be honest. Tell the truth. People can tell when you are sugar coating, spinning the news, or just saying what they want to here. Do not omit – it is the same as lying. People will see that. Half-truths are just as wrong.
2. Take action when needed.
3. Give praise freely when its genuine – it makes you genuine.
4. Do not be afraid to be the first person to endorse something. To step up and say "great!" can take courage. Part of building trust is establishing that you can, and will, stand up and have an opinion even when no one knows what direction the prevailing wind will blow.

5. Be patient. Slower is faster when building trust. It will take time. Let trust build at its own pace.
6. Respect confidentiality. Say it is confidential if you cannot divulge the information. People understand this principal and will respect it, as they know you will keep their information in confidence as well.
7. Admit you do not know if you do not – much better to do this than make up an answer that proves incorrect.
8. Display loyalty. While you may personally disagree with the company line, you must always illustrate and demonstrate your alignment and loyalty to the chain of command and to company policy.
9. Build trust. If you don't trust someone else, ask yourself why. Try to target the reasons why you do not trust and see if you can directly but gently question that person to uncover their masking of the truth before you give up on them completely. In some cases, when a person realizes that you are both able and willing to see through their ruses, they may trust you enough to unmask their façade and show their real self to you.
10. Learn from the mistakes of others.
11. Be open to other points of view. Seeing your actions "your way" will not account for how others see the action undertaken or words spoken. If others perceive your words or actions as untrustworthy, trust will be broken.
12. Be honest. Kickbacks and gifts from vendors must be avoided in total. You must always be beyond any appearance of wrongdoing - well past even looking like anything actually unethical. Nothing breaks trust

like learning someone is receiving gifts. Go beyond what the policy might indicate or require in order to raise the expectation of ethics to a higher level.
13. Last but very importantly – never leak information out of a peer work group without discussing this with the team first. This breaks the circle of trust and damages the team. It also damages the larger organization as the information released will not be messaged correctly or provided within the correct context. Those who routinely leak information should be coached and corrected. This behavior cannot be tolerated.

Takeaways

- ✓ Focus on frequent honest communication with candor
- ✓ Respect confidentiality
- ✓ Listen more than you speak
- ✓ Take the time to message expectations

Exercises

1. Plan frequent meetings with your teams to talk about open concerns.
2. Collect the notes and issues from your teams one-on-ones and use them as discussion points for your team meetings. Always do this anonymously.

17 INTRODUCTION TO PROJECT BASICS AND AVOIDING FAILURE

Learning Objectives:

1. Identify stakeholders up front
2. Write a communication plan
3. Communicate face-to-face
4. Keep the customer involved
5. Over-train the user
6. Institute soft openings rather than grand openings
7. Over-communicate
8. Be honest
9. Trust everyone – and verify everything
10. Write it down

Project management is a science that most of us have learned by doing and coming up through the ranks. This section provides a little insight and guidance to those who are truly brand new to this arena.

"Far better is it to dare mighty things, to win glorious triumphs, even though checkered by failure... than to rank with those poor spirits who neither enjoy nor suffer much, because they live in a gray twilight that knows not victory nor defeat." ~ Theodore Roosevelt

Basic Project Management

If you just take the time to work through these basic principles, you will avoid many problems.

It is common to end up as a project manager through practical experience rather than formal training. Project management is the discipline of completing complex work. A project is comprised of three fundamental elements: scope, budget, and schedule. Understanding what makes up these three elements is crucial for success.

A project is a temporary endeavor. The project and project team have a programmed end. They only exist to produce a unique product once. The challenge of project management is to achieve the desired objective while staying within the bounds of all three elements; scope, schedule, and budget. Remember it only counts as a "win" if the thing you build actually works in the end!

Talent wins games, but teamwork and intelligence wins championships." - Michael Jordan

Stakeholders

"Stakeholder" refers to an individual or group who may be affected by (or perceive itself to be) by a decision, activity, or outcome of a project. Stakeholder management is a critical component to the successful delivery of any project. Stakeholder management creates positive relationships with stakeholders through the appropriate management of their expectations and agreed objectives.

The first step is to identify, recognize, and acknowledge every stakeholder. Determine what the influence and interest is for each of the stakeholders. Use this as the first step in developing a communication plan and a project charter. There are many ways to build trust but the most important is for the project manager to understand each team member and customer individually know what makes them come to work every day and what keeps them worrying at night.

"Plans are worthless. Planning is essential." - Dwight D. Eisenhower

Charters, Planning, and Controls

Start with a charter. A charter is a statement of the scope, objectives, and participants in a project. It provides a preliminary snapshot of roles and responsibilities, lays out the objectives, and identifies key stakeholders. The charter also defines the authority of the project manager as it serves as the reference of authority for the project. A project charter should contain the essence of the project in order to provide a shared understanding, vision, and a common outline of the commitments needed to achieve the objectives within the project team.

A project plan takes everything from the charter and goes deeper into details in all areas. It becomes an outline of the process used by the project team to complete the project. It is sort of the rules of the road. It documents the key aspects of this process including scope, timing, budget, and risk management. The project plan can be viewed as a type of "contract" between the project team members and stakeholders. It sets the process by which the objectives will be achieved, and the responsibilities in carrying out this process. This plan should also dictate how changes, reporting progress, decision-making, and overall approval and spending controls will function.

Project Scope

Project scope is the part of project planning that involves determining and documenting a list of specific project goals, deliverables, features, functions, tasks, deadlines, and ultimately costs. In other words, it is what needs to be achieved and the work that must be done to deliver a project. A project scope statement is a useful tool to outline the project's deliverables and identify the constraints, assumptions and key success factors. The well-written scope statement clearly defines the boundaries of a project.

The scope clearly states what the project is supposed to achieve and what it cannot accomplish. The supporting documents are reviewed to ensure that the project will deliver work in line with the stated goals. The scope that results states the stakeholders' needs and communicates expectations for project performance. This document needs to be completed and validated by the end users before the schedule and the budget can really be understood. Make sure you really understand what the customer needs as early in the project as possible and keep checking that you are doing that and nothing more.

Scope Creep

Scope creep in project management refers to run-away changes or uncontrolled growth of a project's scope after work begins. This happens when the scope of a project is not properly defined or documented at the start of the project. However, it can also happen when the end user specification was never properly developed or when a mechanism to control change orders was never put into pace. Having a charter that outlines what needs to be delivered, and what does not, can help this along with rigorous project controls. Scope creep is the easiest way to blow your budget.

"It takes one woman nine months to have a baby. It cannot be done in one month by impregnating nine women." - unknown

Schedule and Work Breakdown Structure (WBS)

The schedule outlines and communicates all work that needs to be performed. It does so in a manner that describes the tasks, in what order, and identifies the needed resources needed for each step. This outlines the timeframes in which specific sections of work must be performed. The schedule should cover all of the work scope. As with the budget, the schedule needs to cover everything that must be done to make the product functional. An incomplete product in the end that might be on time and budget but does not meet the end user needs is a win for no one.

Without a complete schedule, the project will be difficult to manage, and nearly impossible to deliver on all three elements – budget, schedule, scope.

The building blocks of a schedule start with a Work Breakdown Structure (WBS). The WBS is a hierarchy of all the work need to complete the project in terms of deliverables. This identifies the specific tasks that need to be completed and identifies who actually owns the delivery. These tasks or sections of work are usually called "deliverables." You can see that mapping out all the work and determining who will actually perform each step, and on what timeline, will dovetail into expenses for time, labor, or material.

About Budgets

The budget is the plan or play book of a project. The budget sets financial amounts and limits that are needed for completing the project. Usually, the budget total for a project to be completed is the largest factor in approval of the project rather than schedule. When we combine the specific tasks from the WBS with the budget line item amounts per each deliverable, we can create a view of the monthly budget cash flow and burn rate. A detailed budget sets specific amounts to be spent on a task by task basis. In this way, when one activity appears to be going over the allotted amount, a change order can be created to cover the overage and obtain authorization for additional funds if required.

Burn rate is the rate at which a project is spending money. Typically expressed in monthly terms, it provides a simple basis to understand project cash flow. It can also help understand where the project stands against the budget, scope, and schedule. If one compares the overall percent complete, burn rate, amount of budget remaining, and the items not yet purchased, you can see if you are going to run out of money or time first. It also helps to understand what a 2-3 week delay to an external source might cost you (such as weather).

"The single biggest problem in communication is the illusion that it has taken place." ~ George Bernard Shaw

Communication Plan

Developing a communication plan can help focus your message for stakeholders and team members. Keep the stakeholders informed of problems, but be careful to not let them think you are simply passing on the problem. A well-thought-out plan will make your efforts more efficient, effective, and lasting. If you spend some time planning at the beginning, you can save a great deal of time later on.

Make sure your communications have a purpose. Consider the following goals:

- Announcing project milestone completions
- Recruiting employees to become involved with your project work
- Rallying greater management sponsorship for your project
- Celebrating victories such as safe hours worked
- Countering negativity in social media – a vacuum of information will always generate a negative assumption.
- Dealing with a project crisis that is public knowledge

Steady communications can help with the messaging of bad news. Constant updates on the project course, budget, delays, or what have you are better than watershed type announcements. People love pictures more than words – always remember this in your project communications. Your goal must always be to raise awareness about your project to all stakeholders and perhaps to the larger organization.

Communication is an ongoing tool needed to maintain relationships. An important part of any plan is to continue revising your plan based on your results. Do not skip this step of evaluation and adjustment.

"The most damaging cognitive bias is overconfidence (illusory superiority), making leaders use their "gut" when they should be more rational." - Paul Gibbons

Risk Management

Risk is the possibility that project events will not occur as planned. This is often expressed in any terms of delay (schedule), cost overrun (budget), or creep (scope slippage). Risk can also originate from unplanned events that might occur that will have a negative impact on the project. By studying the possible risk factors before they occur, it is possible to develop countermeasures and contingency plans in advance. Risk management focuses on identifying the risks and ranking their likelihood and severity to the project. Usually the higher-level risk items will have contingency plans developed – the key being that only the most sever and likely risks are mitigated.

No project or activity is risk free. Certain risks might indicate a change in the organization, resources, or project execution plan is required in order to draw in the chances of a bad outcome. Often the budget contingency is predicated on some of the higher risk items discovered. Risk management is not about eliminating risk, but about identifying, assessing, and managing risk. Good risk management increases the likelihood of a successful project.

Safety risks are common on construction projects. Industrial processes that are covered under Process Safety

Management have mature risk management practices – but they are only considered for operating plants.

Some potential events and some common mitigations and contingency actions are as follows:

- Weather. Add some days to the schedule to allow for the likeliness of rain delays in the schedule or for major storm events if they are common to the locality. This will also add to the overall budget as the project will have a certain "burn rate" that is difficult to get out from under for short term delays.

- Project complexity. Very complex projects fail to meet objectives at a higher rate than simple ones. Often consultants will be used to evaluate progress and project preparation and planning at key intervals. Usually the consultants where key members of previous projects similar to the one at hand and may have lived through the problems you faced. They might help plot a better path to avoid possible pitfalls. Learn from them!

- Turnover of Key Staff. Retention bonuses are often used on projects such that key personnel will receive lump sum payments after the project is completed or after a certain number of years. Another countermeasure is to overstaff a project team such that it has some key succession built into the team. For example, a large project might have a very senior project manager and have a senior project manager serving in a supporting role on the team. In this way, there can be a clear and rapid change in leadership without a delay or a change in philosophy.

- Civil Action or Political Unrest. This is very hard to measure and protect against. Those of us who were working during the September 11th attack understand how unrest can trigger staggering delays in projects requiring travel, foreign nationals, and shipping material overseas.

- Bankruptcy of a Key Contractor or Supplier. It is common to bid out material and labor to multiple local or even global suppliers. In this way, if there is a business failure to the supplier or vendor, the entire project is not at stake. With other qualified vendors and contractors already working on the project, it may be possible to expand their scope to fill the gaps rather than starting over. This is common on projects over one billion dollars.

"Those who plan do better than those who do not plan even though they rarely stick to their plan." - Winston Churchill

Avoiding Pitfalls

While projects differ, there are some common threads when it comes to budgets: plan for the worst, plan for the unexpected, and plan on change. Perhaps these are the three great constants in life. Risk management can help identify where changes are likely to come from. Do not forget the contingency in the budget. Contingency in the budget is not to make up for sloppy engineering or weak management – it is included to cover the unknown. There will be unknown.

Here are some tips and practices to help keep you out of trouble:

1. First, find someone to help you! The hardest budget you will ever develop is the first one you are forced to assemble. So for your first budget, get help from an experienced project manager. The same can be said for your first WBS and first schedule.

2. Learn from the most recent projects. If there has been a similar project within the last two years at another plant, try to find out what the budget breakdown was for it. If it was within your company, try to get the budget, schedule, and scope. Set up a phone interview with the project manager or any of the project team that you can locate. No need to reinvent the wheel. Not only can you use what you obtain as a good starting point but you can ask what things went wrong for them as well. Steal like an artist.

3. Ambiguity in scope often leads to unnecessary work and confusion. To avoid this, the scope needs to be clearly defined and to the point. Validate your scope will all the stakeholders.

4. Everything is an estimate. Prepare to change your budget as better estimates and specifications evolve. Project cost always goes up as the detail design increases and the end user specifications become better developed. Personally, I do not believe we ever know any budget amount better than +/- 25%. No one will like this view.

5. Remember contingency. Be realistic when you consider the likelihood of risk. If your project has an 18-month construction window in a region that has

60 or more inches of rain per year, you might need to include the cost of rain delays. If you require extensive piles or foundations how accurate is your geophysical survey?

6. Communicate budget as frequently as you discuss schedule. Keep your team informed of the evolving budget and issues as they surface. Communicate what is expected of them to stay within budget and what is required of them if they have "change orders". This also helps to get your people to focus on controlling costs in areas where they know they will be under budget. We all have a tendency to allow over spending in spots that are not tight. Nevertheless, in the end every dollar counts just the same. This will also help them understand changes and the required change orders as they come up.

7. Set the scope before you lock in the budget. You must ensure that you are actually delivering to the customer a project that works. If there are things not included in the scope needed to make the project work you are doomed to failure. Make sure the customer needs are covered, and the scope is complete. After the scope is locked, you can complete the budget.

8. Manage the scope creep – that is how budgets die. To avoid unplanned work that leads to cost overruns and schedule slips develop a rigorous way to identify "changes" or "change orders" and the impact to delivered cost they bring. Seek additional funding for the project to cover change orders from the right

levels of the organization. Going over budget should not ever be a surprise – the governing body should be approving each change order along with why it is needed and what it adds to cost and time.

9. Do not overlook training or assume that existing operations can deliver the training. Bad training destroys perfect projects. Plan to spend enough on the training.

10. Involve the end user from day one – include this expense in your budget along with any travel or other administrative expenses. This might cost more than you expect if you have to cover the overhead, travel, and salaries. It will be money well spent it in the end.

"Plans are only good intentions unless they immediately degenerate into hard work." - Peter Drucker

Boosting Your Skill Set

The best way to learn about project management is to do it. Most of us that came up through the ranks from operations started out by serving as the "owners representative" or operations stakeholder on smaller projects. We learned by serving junior roles on small projects while being mentored by the more senior engineers, projects, and managers. That is a great way to learn – but not the only one.

In order to become a professional project manager, you must have at least a bachelor's degree in a specific area, such as engineering, chemistry, or computer science, depending on what type of project manager you would like to become.

Beyond the basic technical requirements, most now have a degree in Business Management. The "professional" certification for project management is the PMP. The PMP program itself requires completion of specific hours of project related work and some continuing educational credits.

If you are interested in learning more about being a project manager or working on projects here are a few things to consider doing.

1. Read a book on Agile
2. Read project case studies - many can be found online
3. Pick up a used project management textbook on Amazon - they are dirt cheap used
4. Take some online or night classes on Project Management
5. Talk with your supervisor about getting involved in some of the new or smaller projects within your area - this is the path most of us have taken
6. Volunteer to help with training when any new project comes along – this is a great path to become more connected to the "project delivery" section of your company.

Takeaways:

- ✓ Project Management is a Science
- ✓ Work closely with the end user
- ✓ Communication is the key
- ✓ Schedules need to be obtainable
- ✓ Document the actual customer requirements

- ✓ Never proceed with zero contingency
- ✓ Honesty builds trust
- ✓ Provide frequent unbiased updates rather than sounding alarms later

Exercises

1. What are the three elements of project management?
2. Plan your next family vacation on the dry erase board. Identify who the stakeholders are? What is the scope? Draw out the WBS? How do you control changes? How is this communicated?
3. Define scope creep?
4. What is a change order?
5. Whys is risk management important to projects?
6. What is the last project you were part of or somehow connected to? What went right? What could have been better? What would you have done if you were "in charge"?

Further Reading:

Making Things Happen: Mastering Project Management (Theory in Practice) by Scott Berkun
Project Management For Dummies by Stanley E. Portny
Industrial Megaprojects: Concepts, Strategies, and Practices for Success 1st Edition by Edward W. Merrow
Great Planning Disasters by Peter Geoffrey Hall
To Engineer Is Human: The Role of Failure in Successful Design by Henry Petroski

18 THE VALUE OF BOARD SERVICE

"Everybody talks about the weather, but nobody does anything about it." – Mark Twain

Learning Objectives

1. Serving on a volunteer board can provide professional development
2. Volunteer organizations provide an opportunity to learn leadership influence rather than leadership authority

Volunteering with a nonprofit organization is actually doing something about the weather. If there is a cause you feel is important, take it upon yourself to go out and become part of the solution. Become the change that you want to see.

Supporting a nonprofit organization can take many forms, ranging from donating money, stuffing envelopes, answering phones, passing out literature, or serving on a board of directors. Supporting nonprofits with a one-time or even regular donation is, indeed, a major contribution and is, perhaps, what first comes to mind when the topic of community services arises. Without a doubt, non-profits cannot survive without a robust stable of committed donors. However, supporting through donations of time, labor, and experience might prove to be as much or more valuable to the organization than an actual monetary donation. This is especially true when supporters and volunteers come from the ranks of professionals such as accountants, lawyers, or other specialized skills sets. Without the donations of their time and expertise, the organization would be forced to pay for those services.

"The first and most important choice a leader makes is the choice to serve, without which one's capacity to lead is severely limited." -Robert Greenleaf

For many of us serving on a board of directors enables us to give the benefit of our leadership and strategic skill sets to the organization. By applying these skills in an environment that differs from our normal workplace, we also gain new insights into the value of our skillsets. It's a given that in industry highly specialized skills are expected and are de rigueur for management positions. In the non-profit sector, however, these same skills are often premium skills that a nonprofit can only contract out – or dream about.

But the primary reason you should serve on a nonprofit board is that you want to make the world a better place and you care about the cause. In donating your skills and experience to a nonprofit, you may be surprised at the benefits you will gain.

Potential Development

Patience. You will learn a new level of patience. A group of passionate and committed board members can restate, debate, and iterate for months before reaching a consensus. You will learn patience in order to work through it – it is not the same "work model" nor does it have the same expectations as most of us expect within the private sector. It will stand every manager in good stead to work within this model for a year or two.

Unique Individuals. You will work alongside unique people who will add to your professional and social networks in a way few other opportunities can provide. People who join boards are a wonderful breed. They choose to get off the bench and onto the field. You will be enriched by being in their company.

Negotiation. You will learn to negotiate and function within and from a very different perspective. You will not have the benefit of decision-making authority or traditional motivational "levers" such as salary, promotions, or bonus. You will have only diplomacy and influence.

Community Outreach. You will learn how to leverage the influence and sponsorship of community leaders in order to gain support from the wider community. This requires executive leadership skills of solidifying support.

Teamwork. You will experience a different flavor of teamwork. You will be forced to work on truly cross-functional teams and collaborate more intensely than any private sector I have ever seen. Many of us think of cross-functional teams as a manager, engineering, sales, and maybe a maintenance supervisor. These team members have a single objective and bring a less-than-diverse attitude and ethic to the work. Non-profit boards require you to collaborate on a team made up of, for example, a bank president, lawyer, college professors, doctors, maybe a retired judge, and a few other professions. The team is truly cross-functional and crosses demographics you may have never considered. The very best board members are team-oriented, and the best teams are wide in background and rich in experience. This work provides a learning opportunity everyone should experience.

Solicitation. You will learn to solicit donations. This will change the way you view budgeting forever. Believe me.

Adaptation. You will learn how to run an effective meeting of people who do not work for you and who may have agendas different from your own or perhaps even different from the organizations'. These fellow board members are volunteers, not paid employees, and they may have more business experience than you do.

Innovative Thinking. It will stretch your mind. Board service allows you to bring all of your life experience to the organization and experience the benefit of the balance of a team, which brings all of their experience and insights to share with you.

"In the first place, God made idiots. That was for practice. Then he made school boards." - Mark Twain

Resources and Finding Organizations

In Louisiana, LANO (Louisiana Association of Non-Profit Organization) is a statewide member organization that advocates for the nonprofit community and strengthens the effectiveness of those committed to improving Louisiana. They are the Louisiana "go-to" source for information, tools, resources. LANO can assist you in find training and board openings that fit your skill and interest.

One great educational route into this space is the "Leadership Southwest Louisiana Program," a creation of the SWLA Chamber, develops leaders for the Southwest region who are committed to its advancement. The program begins with an overnight retreat and continues through the year with full day session each month. The experienced-based training sessions are conducted by recognized leaders whose decisions affect the region in areas such as economic development, business, labor, human services, education, law and justice, government, and the media. The content is designed for each participant, capitalizing on leadership skills. The Training increases the individual's knowledge of the community and the state, while encouraging participation in study groups to transfer the skills learned to actual community application. Skills seminars, team building, effective meetings, decision-making, delegating, media relations, organizational communication, community awareness programs, on such issues as the environment, state and local government, educational system, and the judicial system.

"Leadership is not an affair of the head. Leadership is an affair of the heart." -James Kouzes and Barry Posner in The Leadership Challenge

Required Mindset

While serving on a nonprofit board is a great opportunity for you to learn and grow, I would recommend everyone consider the following factors.

Do you care enough about the cause? Do you have passion for what the organization does? Are you willing to work on the activity for a year, or two, or three? Think about your commitment to the cause itself.

Do you have the time necessary to fulfill your commitment? The ideal board member is not only eager to serve, but also has the ability to participate in meetings and events. The commitment could range from a few half days a month or more depending on the organization and expectations. Those who are in the earlier periods of their careers or with new families may not have that time available.

Do you have a commitment to stewardship or servant leadership? Serving a nonprofit as a board member is dependent not only whether you are willing to commit the time but also if you are willing to drive an endeavor that is a "for others" and not a "for me" path.

Are you a good listener? Are you willing to listen and work toward consensus? Everyone who volunteers as a board member is likely to be a community leader in some capacity. Effective board work requires recognizing other members have good ideas, building on all of the ideas rather than capitalizing on a single path, and building consensus rather than majority.

Are you willing to roll up your sleeves and go into the trenches when the time comes to support the actual work? Are you able to assist with the annual fundraiser or events throughout the year? Activities will vary from organization to organization – some of them will require you to get your hands dirty. Just ask yourself if that is an activity you will enjoy. It might be the best fun you have ever had!

Are you certain that joining the board will not create a conflict of interest with your career, employer, or your spouse? Most employers, and many boards, will request you to submit a declaration stating what you are doing, identify any potential conflict of interests, and request an accounting of your time out of the office. Make sure that those whom you work closely with and your family members know the commitment you are considering. Their support will enhance your experience as a board member. Their lack of support could easily sabotage your good intentions.

"Servant leadership is all about making the goals clear and then rolling your sleeves up and doing whatever it takes to help people win. In that situation, they don't work for you; you work for them." -Ken Blanchard

Closing

Consider joining a non-profit organization in order to support a cause you feel strongly about. You will gain back multifold what you give and make the world a better place.

"We make a living by what we get. We make a life by what we give." -Winston Churchill

Exercises:

1. List out the volunteer organizations that you might have an interest working with.
2. Do you know the directors of those organizations? Find them.
3. Determine if you can make the time commitment to volunteer to work with those organizations

4. Seek out a board position if you have volunteered with them and are sure you are aligned with their mission and execution

19 BREAKING YOUR BAD HABITS BEFORE THEY BUST YOUR CAREER

Learning Objectives:

1. What are the big ten negative behaviors
2. Small changes in behavior make a big difference over time
3. It is up to you

Introduction

"The best cure for one's bad tendencies is to see them in action in another person." - Alain de Botton

Every one of us has some bad work habits. Maybe we procrastinate, are critical, gossip, or lack punctuality. These behaviors can reflect poorly upon you, and can even cost you your next promotion. In some cases, they might even get you fired. One bad habit is not likely to get you fired but the cumulative effect overtime is going to negatively affect your career. It sets a bad "brand" for your professional identity. So consider these thoughts and take a self-inventory of where you are and where you think you should be.

The "Big Ten"

"I never could have done what I have done without the habits of punctuality, order, and diligence, without the determination to concentrate myself on one subject at a time. – Charles Dickens

1. Not Being Present. Do not be the person who is using his laptop or phone during a meeting rather than paying attention. You will miss something, you are not providing input, and it is rude. If you have an urgent business or personal matter, it is better to excuse yourself then to leap out every 15 minutes with another phone call. If you are in a meeting, be in the meeting – do not multitask. Simple. Do not do it.

"I have never seen anyone drink themselves smart, successful, or happy." - Unknown

2. Alcohol. Do not be the person who gets a tipsy at the Christmas party. This demonstrates a low level of self-control, disciple, and poor professional judgement. Likewise, if you drank too much the night before it is 100% better to call in sick then show up hung over.

"Almost every successful person begins with two beliefs: the future can be better than the present, and I have the power to make it so." – David Brooks

3. Negativity. Repeatedly being the Negative-Nancy at every suggestion or new initiative makes you appear resistant to change or not being a team player. Being contrary, pessimistic or always having a bad attitude can be construed as being uncooperative and not supportive of the company mission. Preface your questions like; 'I think it's a great idea, I fully support

it, when we reach step B how will we proceed?" That is much better messaging of your true position. Take the time to message your intent and emotions clearly. Never refer to things as being "Deal breakers" or use phrases like "That won't work", or "We don't have resources for that", or its too big or too hard. (Maybe it is just too big FOR YOU). All of those comments and behaviors make you look unsupportive, negative, and not willing to engage. When it actually is a concept that pushes you further than you can reach, voicing it will only make you look unprofessional. So wait and think out what you should do and how you can approach the situation rather than just being negative. After you have thought it out, go and discuss with your manager, or peers in a constructive, thoughtful, respectful, positive manner. This is a critical behavior for you to be viewed as a promotable candidate. Practice this path - become the peer people go to when they want to bounce an idea off you that might break through a roadblock.

4. Office Romance. All I can say here is avoid dating people you work with. Do not do it. It is a career-limiting move and could be enough to keep you from being promoted in many organizations. Human Resources will weigh the potential future risk of a harassment charge around a past relationship as too risky for you to be a candidate. It also speaks to the possibility that you will engage in another complicating relationship that better judgement would tell you to avoid. Join a dating site, go to a

church singles group, or take a continuing education night class - do not use the office for dating.

"Whoever fights monsters should see to it that in the process he does not become a monster. And if you gaze long enough into an abyss, the abyss will gaze back into you." - Friedrich Nietzsche

5. Gifts and Entertainment. Not only must you always function 100% above board with regard to expense reports, gifts, and entertainment. You also must ALWAYS APPEAR BEYOND REPROACH. Sometimes that means you lean a little past what the company policy might allow. Never allow yourself to even appear to be swayed by "perks" from contractors, vendors, or other business stakeholders. Do not get sucked into this career-limiting trap. Do not let endless vendor lunches become the hallmark of your career - the exceptions being those in sales, media, and marketing.

"The while we keep a man waiting, he reflects on our shortcomings." – Unknown French proverb

6. Punctuality. Being late for work functions, commitments, meetings, or just late coming in the office will get you branded as a low performer. It does not matter if you work until 10:00 every night – if you are 5 minutes late every morning you will stick out to everyone - your boss, your peers, and worst your own team. Same goes for being always the last one in the meeting room before the door shuts – or even not being ready once the meeting starts. Do not be the person who has to rifle through his notes

or turn his computer on before you start the meeting. Do not be that person. Punctuality counts and it is a career limiting habit.

'Never fail to know that if you are doing all the talking, you are boring somebody.' – Helen Gurley

7. Do not "make-stuff-up". If you do not know something or you are not prepared to discuss just say it. Do not make up some excuse or half-baked response. Never tell a lie. Never tell a half-truth. When you find yourself in this predicament, if you must say something, remember these options a) I do not know and I will find out, b) I do know that status and it will be rolled out at x time, or c) share what you do know if you can.

Never talk to hear yourself. Never sound like a used car salesman. Be sincere and honest – when you are not everyone can see through it all the time. No one wants to have this fellow on their team – do not be him. No one wants to work for him, with him, or have them on their team.

"If we didn't have deadlines, we'd stagnate." Walt Disney

8. Missing Deadlines. When you miss a deadline, you are saying that you work slow, are bogged down in details, cannot manage your time, unable to delegate, estimate efforts incorrectly. No matter how you look at it, if you are consistently missing your deadlines and commitment dates you are freezing yourself into your current level in the

organization. If you have three assignments that you are working on, make sure you hit one dead on and make a good showing on the others – missing all of them because you tried to "home run" all of them is a rookie failure. Focus on making good base hits consistently. To protect yourself from this dangerous trap think about; using the 80/20 rule, saying "no" to optional assignments, and adjusting your internal measure closer to "good-enough" over perfection.

"The amount of "followers" you have does not make you better than anyone else. Hitler had millions. Jesus had twelve." – Mark Hart

9. Pleasing Everyone. There is no place for pleasing everyone in business. Leadership positions are where tough decisions have to be made. Many of them will not be popular – do not let yourself be paralyzed by the fear of not making the popular decision. Be fair, be transparent, be honest – but also be decisive. People will respect your choices and your judgement even if they are disappointed from time to time.

10. Abusing Time Off. Do not abuse time off from work that is allowed by your company policy. You know what is reasonable and that is where you should self-govern your use of days. You might very well be allowed more paid time off by policy but do you want to be labeled as the "milk-the-system" person? Use common sense and demonstrate to your peers and your team that you respect the principals in play rather than using all of something you are allowed.

Key Takeaways:

- ✓ You are writing your own history every day
- ✓ Every day you are interviewing for your next position within
- ✓ Small changes made overtime can make a giant impact in the long run

Exercises

1. Write down the key success factors for your current position. Ask a peer who you trust to do the same thing and compare notes. What is your list missing?

Further Reading:

The Harada Method the Spirit of Self-Reliance by Takashi Harada and Norman Bodek

20 AVOIDING JOB BURN OUT

Learning Objectives

1. Everyone has stress
2. Stress impacts all of us
3. It is important to learn to manger your stress rather than just survive it

Before You Skip This!

Some of you will skip this section – please do not. If you read nothing else consider the following:

- You have a stress bank account – you only have a set balance, when you over draw bad things happen to your relationships, career, and your health. Keep tabs on this and do not over draft.
- There are things you can do for yourself that will provide a stronger foundation for your emotional stability and improve your chances of working through periods of high stress.
- There are entire books if not complete libraries that deal with establishing and maintaining healthy work life balance – it is worth your time, and will aid your professional development, to become familiar with this entire subject.

Introduction

Job burnout is the result of work related stress and pressure. It is a form of emotional and physical fatigue that can lead to more serious depression as well as serious health issues overtime. Not only can this reduce you job satisfaction and happiness, diminish your actual work performance, but it might also affect your relationships outside of the workplace. It is something to take seriously.

To see where you stand please ask yourself the following questions. This is not scientific and I am not a doctor – these questions are based on my own observations and direct experience.

"I tell the kids, somebody's gotta win, somebody's gotta lose. Just don't fight about it. Just try to get better." Yogi Berra

Where Do You Stand?

Take a minute to walk through these questions.

1. Has it been longer than six months since your last vacation?
2. Has your doctor diagnosed you as being "Pre-Hypertensive" or have you had borderline high blood pressure?
3. Have you had more than one speeding ticket this year or other moving violation?
4. Have you been in a "fender bender" this year?
5. Have you been late for more than three important meetings or engagements in the last two weeks?
6. Have you lost your drive at work – do you feel you are just rolling with the punches and fighting fires from day to day?
7. Have you missed an important family event this month?
8. You do not feel motivated at work. You have difficulty focusing or exhibit a short attention span.

9. Have you eaten more than four meals in front of a computer screen this week?
10. Have you slept less than 6 hours a night more than once this week?
11. Are you sick more often than your coworkers?
12. Have you stopped your former exercise regimen?

If you have answered yes to more than 3-4 of these you are headed for trouble. Sit back and consider your answers – are you becoming the person you really want to be?

"We are here to laugh at the odds and live our lives so well that Death will tremble to take us." Charles Bukowski

Root Causes

There can be many factors that lead to job burn out. Occupational burnout is thought to result from long-term, unresolvable job stress. Everyone will have different triggers and coping mechanisms to manage stress levels. Scholarly research suggests six risk factors for burnout: mismatch in workload, mismatch in control, lack of appropriate awards, loss of a sense of positive connection with others in the workplace, perceived lack of fairness, and conflict between values. Perhaps explain a bit better in laymen's terms some of the common root causes are listed as follows:

1. Unreasonable differences between your work resources and the expectations placed upon you to complete assignments.
2. Confusion in the work place as to your degree of authority
3. Unclear about what your supervisor or other team mates expect from you
4. Different performance expectations from your peers

5. Feeling undermined by your colleagues or by another department such as Human Resources
6. Management that may second guess your decisions or check all of your work
7. Continued threat or likelihood of lay off or termination

"I have come here to chew bubble gum and kick ass, and I'm all out of bubble gum." Roddy Piper as Nada in They Live (1988)

Working Through It

Unfortunately, there really is no cure. Burn out is a condition that we need to manage. While there are many sources of burn out, they impact individuals differently, there are also different paths for recovery. The important thing is that you address the problem rather than let it build and become worse.

1. Talk to your supervisor about your feelings and see what they can do to help you.

2. Take an extended vacation if you can – if you can.

3. Support systems are an important component of stress management. Your spouse, family, friends, and coworkers are pivotal in managing stress. Talk daily, listen daily, and support each other. Quantity over quantity when it comes to relationships - better to have a few deep friendships than many people you are only familiar with. Everyone is different in

the way the share and support each other - find you way and do not try to "go it alone".

4. Contact your companies Employee Assistance Program (EAP) for help.

5. Set aside time in your day to relax – schedule an hour with no activity planned. Really. Try it for a few weeks.

6. Set up an appointment with your regular physician – sit down and talk with them about what is going on with work, stress, sleep, exercise. You might be run down a bit from a health problem of which you are unaware.

7. Get a pet. Dogs are great.

8. Listing. Write down the items you are worried about in a notebook. Develop simple action plans to remove the stressors. Often simply writing down the item can help define the scope – often this reduces the stress in total. Often knowing that it is written down so as not to be lost can alleviate a great deal of stress. Try it, this works wonders for me.

9. Be honest. If you have a mismatch in values with your current employer perhaps, it is time to leave. Why be unhappy forever? If your values differ from the way your employer does business maybe it is time to move on with your career. Why should you always be fighting city hall?

10. Start walking everyday – even 30 minutes every morning can help clear the mind and shake off the morning I-dread-going-to-work feeling.

11. Do you have a poor job fit? Are you under too much strain to "stretch" past where you really can do the job? If your employer is putting you in this space are you really with the right organization.

12. Take up a new hobby or volunteer with a non-profit in your area. I know it will sound counter intuitive but often helping others can help you unwind yourself.

13. Start spending time with your family and not-at-work friends. Being isolated socially might be making you feel more stressed.

"If you end up with a boring miserable life because you listened to your mom, your dad, your teacher, your priest, or some guy on television telling you how to do your shit, then you deserve it." – Frank Zappa

Takeaways

- ✓ People who feel in control (have an internal locus of control) have a better mental outlook and are able to handle stress more effectively (and are able to avoid or manager burn out)
- ✓ Work with your supervisor on this – they may have noticed a drop off in performance or change in attitude and would be more supportive and helpful if they understood your situation

- ✓ Job burn out will happen to everyone at some point – manage the issue before it overcomes you

Exercises:

1. Think about exercise – consider walking every day. It will greatly improve your mental well-being. If you are physically able to engage in more active exercise that is great – but pick something that can become part of your daily routine.

2. General Health. If it has been more than a year since your last routine physical schedule an exam with your doctor.

3. Check on your retirement plan and life insurance. Often finances are a source of stress and pressure behind the scenes – know that you have a retirement plan in action and that your family will be taken care of in the event of your untimely passing can significantly reduce your stress level.

Further Reading:

Stress Management For Dummies by Allen Elkin
The 7 Habits of Highly Effective People: Powerful Lessons in Personal Change by Stephen R. Covey

21 DO I WANT A JOB OR A CAREER

Learning Objectives

1. What makes up a job
2. How is a career different
3. What can you do for your own career development
4. Actions that you need to avoid

Job Dissatisfaction: Modern Plague of the Work Place

Today, job satisfaction seems the exception rather than the rule. Let us face it, no matter how talented you are, or how positive you try to be, everyone suffers satisfaction issues from time to time. This can cause many employees, at all levels, to become disengaged. Nothing will sink your organization faster than disengaged leaders. Disengagement kills creativity & productivity, skyrockets absenteeism and can drive many individuals into actual depression. When we are unhappy at work, those emotions have a way of infiltrating all aspects of our lives, and this can often cause family issues, relationship problems, and other more serious life issues.

Sometimes dissatisfaction is based on a work-life balance issue, being passed over for a promotion, not earning what you are worth, or with your career advancement. It's so very easy to fall into a downward spiral of "disengagement". Let us have some candor on this point. Once you are pulled into this morass, it is hard to recover, it is emotionally draining, leads to depression, and influences the quality of your work. In some cases, this can start a negative feedback loop. When you are unhappy and become disengaged, this decreases your productivity and might eventually garner negative attention from supervision. This negative attention will only augment your unhappiness and dissatisfaction at work - the career death spiral. A great manager can see this and help you out of the spiral, but sometimes you might have to figure your own way out. Let us talk about the root cause of the disappointment.

Often all of this stems from the differences between your "work life" and your "career expectations". Sometimes we have arrived at expectations that are not realistic or are at least a mismatch with the actual job that we hold. In other words, your work does not match your expectations. The most common mismatch is to have expectations suited to a "career" when you actually are working in a "job". Let us take a moment to discuss jobs versus careers.

"If you want to achieve greatness stop asking for permission" - unknown

Jobs

Jobs come and jobs go. A job is just there to pay your rent. Jobs can be either short term or long term. A job is simply something you do to earn money, purely transactional. Career advancement is not something you care about in a job. The work often does not have to interest you at all. A job has minimal impact on future resumes and job applications because it is completely unrelated to the positions you will be applying for in the future. It is simply what you are doing in exchange for pay. A career is a series of profoundly related jobs that will always be used on future applications and resumes.

A job offers very few networking opportunities because the people with whom you interact are not people you will likely know in a future position. A career is loaded with networking opportunities, as most of the people around you are involved in similar careers to yours and they will keep popping up repeatedly.

At a typical job, your goal is usually just to get the task done and not annoy the boss. All you really want from a job is a regular paycheck and a positive reference from the boss, and all you have to do to get that done is to get your tasks completed and stay out of the way.

This means that you should not be investing significant emotional energy into the job. Just do what you are supposed to do with the minimum amount of expended mental, physical, and emotional energy, and save that energy for other endeavors.

If your employment situation sounds more like a job than a career, do one of two things. Accept it. Does it provide you income, insurance, and stability for your family? If that is what you need and what you have, then manage your expectations and accept your position. This is a better situation than most people find themselves in and it might be good enough for you. You should be doing the tasks that are required and conserving your life for the other things - family, hobbies, and other callings. If it is not what you want, then we need to talk about having a "career".

"Satisfaction lies in the effort, not in the attainment, full effort is full victory" – Mahatma Gandhi

Careers

Careers are a long-term investment of your youth, your life, energy, and college tuition - of all that is aimed at a progression of achievement. Careers are a calling towards a certain professional area, like being a doctor, a chef, a teacher, or some specific professional role that has personal emotional appeal. They are deeply connected with your personal values. Your career may be your "brand" or your mission in life. This "career" is a series of connected employment opportunities; sometimes these are actually a collection of "jobs" in the beginning, which build up your toolbox of skills. As your skills increase and you have opportunities to demonstrate your mastery of the basics, more opportunities to advance into higher paying and higher prestige employment opportunities will present themselves later on. These progressive steps provide greater responsibility, higher income, and more challenging problems to tackle. A career provides the path of experiences and growth that will propel your professional life. Maybe it is your life.

In a career, your goal is to not just "getting it done". Your goal must be to build a skillset, to demonstrate your capability, and to learn more at every point along the way. Aim not just to complete the task but also to better yourself. You must strive to learn new skills, gain deeper experience, build your professional network, and slowly broaden the foundation of your position. These actions will put you on a trajectory for advancement, greater compensation, and perhaps even make you a candidate for more senior positions with other organizations.

Saving Your Life

If you are trapped in a job but desire a career, what are you options? If you want growth within your professional area and advancement, you should push hard for a career. This means investing emotional energy into your career and pursuing useful resume building experiences even when they are very difficult and stressful. You may need to make a transition between companies in order to achieve this; you might have to do this several times. You have to "own" your professional development and you will likely have to reach a level of achievement and recognition, before you are seen as "human capital" that should be mentored and developed. That does not mean you have to give up on work-life balance. It means setting some milestones for your professional development, mapping out where you want to go, what is needed to get you there, and what tools you need. Beyond all else, you must own it yourself and go do it!

You must be accountable for your development and in a sense become the owner of the "career" that your employer is not fulfilling. This can take on many shapes and directions. Develop a long-term career aspirations plan. Hope is not a plan - make a plan and think big. This is your career development plan – plot out what you want to achieve.

Do not base this on building income, but instead base it on your dreams. Do not base your plan on how much money you can make. Base it on your long-term life goals and job satisfaction. Explore your strengths. Be honest about your weaknesses. Break up that big goal into several shorter term "achievable" action items. Set some milestones around these and then make a point to celebrate them along the way. Consider going back to school, online or at night. You might benefit from meeting with some very effective third party career coaches. Ask your line manager for on-the-job training opportunities and ask specifically for any stretch assignments.

"The truth is that our finest moments are most likely to occur when we are feeling deeply uncomfortable, unhappy, or unfulfilled. For it is only in such moments, propelled by our discomfort, that we are likely to step out of our ruts and start searching for different ways or truer answers." - M. Scott Peck

Find a mentor if you do not have one. A senior level professional who can offer you advice can become very valuable. Network yourself to death. Make a point of adding every contact you have, or ever have had, to your LinkedIn network. Join discussion groups relevant to your professional area and become a regular contributor. Set some monthly goals for increasing your network size.

Read the book "Thanks for the Feedback: The Science and Art of Receiving Feedback" by Douglas Stone and Sheila Heen. Take calculated risks. Do not be afraid to fail often along the way. It is not how many times you fall, but how many times you are willing to get back up that count.

There are general points you should consider.

1. Have a realistic view of promotions. You might work for 2-3 years, or longer depending on your profession, as an individual contributor. If you have

had a promotion or even two actual increases in responsibility, that event could put you into a holding pattern for a long time. This is not bad – this is the period where you establish a solid record of accomplishment, of being a solid performer. There will be a point you reach where you will not be promoted, but rather will be assigned specific projects of importance. This is how careers are built.

2. Look for the light at the end of the tunnel. Is there a clear opportunity in the next 1-2 years to move into another position? It might be best just to ride this out. Hard advice to give and harder to take – sometimes you just have to push your way through the work, unhappy as it might be.

3. Resist the urge to break the chain-of-command and complain to your line supervisor's manager directly. This is always 100% guaranteed to identify you as one who is not able to follow directions and does not follow the chain-of-command. Demonstrating this behavior will lock you into the current position you are in and might even identify you with the company as a troublemaker. You do not want this – so do not do it.

4. Do not quit. I have seen many people leave a company only to move into a more adverse work situation. Never leave a job if you do not already have another one accepted, have passed the physical, signed the offer, and been vetted out through the background check. I have seen firsthand

people leave prematurely and become stranded between positions. Be careful.

5. No ghosting. This merits its own bullet point. Never, never, leave a job by simply disappearing. Always give notice, two weeks or more, depending on the situation, your supervisor might let you leave on good terms with less notice. Nevertheless, always provide at least two weeks notice. Ghosting will stick with you in the industry, and if even done once, can wreck your career.

6. Stay at least two years. When you are interviewing a giant red flag to your potential manager is multiple job or company changes, ones that are not promotions, and that happen every two years or more often. If you have two or three of these moves in a row, you will be avoided for "career" positions and will continue to be pulled into "job" positions.

In closing, consider if you are in a job or a career. If you only need or want a job - work it like a job. No need to grind yourself into the ground. If you want a career, but are stuck in a "job", it might be time to move on, take ownership of your own career growth, or possibly both.

"If you don't feel it, flee from it. Go where you are celebrated, not merely tolerated" - Paul F. Davis

Takeaways

- ✓ Your expectations might not match the reality of where you are

- ✓ Try to hang in there and make the most of a bad situation
- ✓ Do not jump from the frying pan to the fire
- ✓ Work with your manager
- ✓ Do not break rank to complain
- ✓ Be careful to not have too many job moves that are not clear promotions

Exercises:

1. Think out and write down what you want to achieve in your career. What are the requirements in terms of experience, education, and skill sets?

2. Perform a gap analysis between what you want in item #1 and where you are right now in your career. Are there gaps? Break them into a four square – Big or small and critical or nice to have. See where you stand. If you want to be a Vice President, you might need to have an MBA – that would be critical and big. Fill this out as best as you can and review with a mentor.

Big		
Small		
	Nice to have	Critical

3. Map out how you will achieve the growth outlines in #2 with some durations and actions. Apply some timeline to these actions. Sit with a mentor and review your plans. Just because you have a few big and critical gaps to work on does not mean your goal

is impossible – it only means you will need a good plan to reach your goal!

Further Reading:

Winning by Jack Welch
Thanks for the Feedback: The Science and Art of Receiving Feedback by Douglas Stone and Sheila Heen

22 CONCLUSION

"Do the difficult things while they are easy and do the great things while they are small. A journey of a thousand miles must begin with a single step."- Lao Tzu

Thank you for indulging me with your time. I hope some of this was useful to you.

Always communicate with candor and honesty; this is the base for most of what this book has outlined. Communication is about the receiver hearing it – not about the sender being heard. Be professional in your conduct and treatment of others at work as well as away from work. You always represent your organization no matter what the time or location.

Leading people is about holding them up and carrying them along at times – not about pushing them ahead. Make an effort to get off on the right foot when you can. The surest way to raise yourself in an organization is to make a habit of lifting up your team and improving those around you.

Become a lifter and not a climber. Collaborate. Work together. Bolster and build your emotion intelligence. Those who succeed often do so by being the glue that holds the smart people together – rarely are they the brilliant individuals. Work on becoming that glue.

Make yourself a lifelong learner and from time to time take account of where you are, where you want to be, and formulate a plan to make it to that place. Set goals. Make them challenging. Do not be afraid when you miss them. Plan. Adapt. Try. Try again.

Please reach out to me on LinkedIn with any feedback and feel free to join my network. I would be happy to connect with you.

Peace to all.

Made in the USA
Columbia, SC
14 December 2020